THE PARADOXICON

THE PARADOXICON

NICHOLAS FALLETTA

John Wiley & Sons, Inc.
New York • Chichester • Brisbane • Toronto • Singapore

First published by Doubleday & Company, Inc. in 1983.
John Wiley & Sons, Inc., edition published 1990.

Library of Congress Cataloging-in-Publication Data

Falletta, Nicholas L.
The paradoxicon.

Bibliography: p. 203
Includes index.
I. Paradox. I. Title.
ISBN 0-471-52950-8

PRINTED IN THE UNITED STATES OF AMERICA
90 91 10 9 8 7 6 5 4 3 2 1

For information about our audio products, write us at:
Newbridge Book Clubs, 3000 Cindel Drive, Delran, NJ 08370

For permission to reprint copyrighted material, grateful acknowledgment is made to the following sources:

Harry N. Abrams, Inc.: Figure 58, *Sleeping Venus Uncovered by Amor*, by Henry Kettle, and Figure 59, *Castle*, by J. W. Schwenck, from *Hidden Images*, by Fred Leeman, Joost Elffers, and Mike Schuyt. Photographs by Mike Schuyt. Copyright © 1976 by Harry N. Abrams. Reproduced by permission of Harry N. Abrams, Inc.

Beeldrecht/Vaga: Figure 18, *Drawing Hands;* Figure 20, *Day and Night;* Figure 21, *Circle Limit IV;* Figure 22, *Belvedere;* Figure 24, *Ascending and Descending;* Figure 38, *Waterfall;* Figure 61, *High and Low;* Figure 62, *Other World;* Figure 63, *Relativity;* Figure 86, *Möbius Strip, II;* Figure 112, *Square Limit*—all by M. C. Escher. Copyright © Beeldrecht, Amsterdam/Vaga, New York. Collection Haags Gemeentemuseum, The Hague.

Bobbs-Merrill Educational Publishing: Excerpts on pages 197 and 201–2 from *Zeno's Paradoxes*, by Wesley Salmon, editor. Copyright © 1970 by Bobbs-Merrill Educational Publishing.

Paul Curry: Figure 33, "The disappearing rabbit paradox." Copyright © 1955 by Paul Curry.

Martin Gardner: Figure 49, "Cantor's diagonal method," and excerpt on pages 65–66 from "The Hierarchy of Infinities and the Problems It Spawns." Published in *Scientific American*, March 1966. Copyright © 1966 by Martin Gardner. Figure 71, "The paradox of the second ace," from "Probability Paradoxes" in *Mathematical Puzzles and Diversions*. Published by Simon and Schuster. Copyright © 1959 by Martin Gardner.

For Betty Ann

ACKNOWLEDGMENTS

Although writing a book is by nature a solitary activity, no one writes a book alone. I would like to acknowledge the contributions made by the following people. I would like to thank Jeanette Cissman, who did all the line drawings and who coordinated all the other elements of the art program for this book. Without her expert help, it would have been impossible for me to complete this project. I also want to thank Mary Reid and Toby Wertheim for their help with much of the library research. Thanks also go to Dan Schiller, Beth Murphy, Carolyn Quinn, Ned Levy, and others who passed along useful information over the years. The following people read drafts of the manuscript and made helpful suggestions: Jane Driscoll, Ellen Rosenbush, Susan McMahon, Morton Davis, and Marilyn Davis. Special thanks go to Martin Gardner for clarifying the surprise ace paradox in the chapter on "Probability Paradoxes." I would also like to give special thanks to my sister Denise Mazza, who greatly simplified the logistics of writing, and to Peyton Moss, Georgie Remer, and others at Doubleday who assisted in the publication of this book. Special thanks to Steve Ross and others at John Wiley & Sons for their interest in this book. Most of all, I thank my wife, Betty Ann, for her encouragement and perseverance.

N. Falletta
April 1990

CONTENTS

LIST OF FIGURES

INTRODUCTION

This book was written for the general reader who has an interest in paradoxes but who does not have a technical background in mathematics, logic, science, or philosophy. The paradoxes discussed in this book are drawn from these disciplines and from others; and, although many of these problems involve sophisticated concepts and logical reasoning, none of them requires the reader to have previous knowledge of anything beyond ordinary language and simple arithmetic. This collection is intended to represent the diversity of the paradoxer's intelligence and imagination; however, it is by no means comprehensive. Numerous other paradoxes—many as interesting as these and some more complex—have been excluded because of space limitations or because of their technical demands.

This book contains twenty-five chapters arranged alphabetically by title. I chose the alphabetical organization over a historical or thematic one, because it seemed the most appropriate in its simplicity and appeal for a collection as diverse as this one. Each chapter is intended to stand on its own; thus, it is possible to read the book in any sequence. At the end of each chapter is a parenthetical note indicating other related chapters in the book.

A paradox has been described whimsically as "truth standing on its head to attract attention." This statement probably comes closer to capturing the essence of a paradox than any formal definition that can be offered, for, in fact, a paradox is a very difficult thing to pin down.

The word itself comes from the Greek (*para* and *doxos*), meaning "beyond belief." As used today, the term "paradox" covers a range of meanings, with its most general reference being to any statement or belief that is contrary to expectation or received opinion. The definitions of paradox which are relevant to this book are somewhat more specific, involving basically three different meanings: (1) a statement that appears contradictory but which is, in fact, true; (2) a statement that appears true but which, in fact, involves a contradiction; and (3) a valid or good argument that leads to contradictory conclusions. Obviously, the two types of paradoxical statements identified in (1) and (2) are often, though not always, the conclusions of the arguments identified in (3). This book is chiefly concerned with arguments—whether they be visual, logical, mathematical, scientific, or otherwise—that attempt to sustain paradoxical conclusions.

Some paradoxes are profound and some are trivial. Many paradoxes turn out to be fallacies, but even this eventuality does not necessarily make them trivial. It is often the case that fallacious paradoxes point the way to major reconstructions of the systems they involve. Of course, not all paradoxes are fallacious; some are well reasoned but nevertheless involve counterintuitive notions. In these paradoxes, the conclusions we are forced to accept *are* true, but they seem to be unexpected and contrary to common sense. As Anatol Rapoport, a communications expert and game theorist, notes in "Escape from Paradox" (*Scientific American*, July 1967):

> Paradoxes have played a dramatic part in intellectual history, often foreshadowing revolutionary developments in science, mathematics, and logic. Whenever, in any discipline, we discover a problem that cannot be solved within the conceptual framework that supposedly should apply, we experience shock. The shock may compel us to discard the old framework and adopt a new one. It is to this process of intellectual molting that we owe the birth of many of the major ideas in mathematics and science. . . . Zeno's paradox of Achilles and the tortoise gave birth to the idea of convergent infinite series. Antinomies (internal contradictions in mathematical logic) eventually blossomed into Gödel's theorem. The paradoxical result of the Michelson-Morley experiment on the speed of light set the stage for the theory of relativity. The discovery of the wave-particle duality of light forced a reexamination of deterministic causality, the very foundation of scientific philosophy, and led to quantum mechanics. The paradox of Maxwell's demon, which Leo Szilard first found a way to resolve in 1929, gave impetus more recently to the profound insight that the seemingly disparate concepts of information and entropy are intimately linked to each other.

It is possible to add numerous other paradoxes to Rapoport's list of those that have produced significant changes in the way we see the world. As Willard V. Quine has noted, "Of all the ways of paradoxes, perhaps the quaintest is their capacity on occasion to turn out to be so very much less frivolous than they look."

Regardless of their type, paradoxes tend to exhibit several characteristics. Chief among these is contradiction, but self-reference and vicious circularity are often present, too. Paradoxes generally possess a good measure of ambiguity, and their solutions frequently involve sorting out various meanings or interpretations embedded in the ordinary language or images that form them. A paradoxer must keep a sharp eye out for ambiguity, vagueness, and other signs of fallacious reasoning.

A historical survey of paradoxes in Western culture shows that there have been three periods of intense interest in paradoxical thinking. The first occurred in ancient Greece, from about the fifth to the second century B.C. The liar paradox and the paradoxes of Zeno can be traced to this period. Interest in paradoxes seems to have faded sometime before the birth of Christ, and it was not until medieval scholastics rediscovered classical texts that a revival of interest in "insoluble" problems began. The seeds of interest planted by the medieval scholastics bloomed during the Renaissance. More than five hundred collections of paradoxes—ranging from scientific to literary—are known to have been published in Western Europe during this period.

The third period of interest in paradoxes began in the second half of the nineteenth century and continues to the present day. It was between the mid-1800s and the early 1900s that much of the formalization of mathematics and logic was achieved, and this inevitably led to a consideration of paradoxes, some new and some very old and still unsolved. In addition to the prestigious position paradox gained in mathematics and logic, its reputation in science was enhanced by the counterintuitive upheavals resulting from relativity theory and quantum mechanics.

The trend continues today into other areas of intellectual activity including psychology, economics, political science, and philosophy, as well as in the arts. It is a trend which already has produced the most extensive and rigorous commentaries about paradoxes in history. Based on the ability of paradoxes to dazzle us by bringing us to the limits of human thought and perception, it seems likely that contemporary interest in them is more than just a passing intellectual fad.

THE PARADOXICON

AMBIGUOUS FIGURES

An ambiguous figure is one that can be interpreted as two or more different images. Do you see a beautiful, young woman or an ugly, old hag? Can you see both images—at the same time?

The figure of the young-old woman was designed by the American psychologist E. G. Boring. It achieves its effect by forcing us to perceive the figure as fluctuating between two sharply contrasted

1. Boring's young-old woman figure.

images. The reversibility of the figure is caused by the careful placement of lines that function in two different visual contexts. The significance of these ambiguous lines changes as our eyes scan the picture. For example, as we shift our gaze downward from the cheek and jawbone of the young woman, the same lines become the old lady's large, hooked nose. Similarly, the young woman's neck-band becomes the old woman's mouth.

The young-old woman drawing involves a figure-ground reversal; that is, at any given moment, only one image may dominate as the "figure" while the rest of the image serves as the background. Although shifting your eyes will facilitate the reversal of the images, it is entirely unnecessary to do so. If you stare blankly at the image, it will reverse spontaneously.

Probably the most famous figure-ground reversal was designed by the Danish psychologist Edgar Rubin. It involves an ambiguous figure which may be interpreted as a pair of profiles looking at each other or as a vase, which is formed by the space between the profiles (Figure 2). According to Rubin, "The reader has the opportunity not only to convince himself that the ground is perceived

2. Rubin's vase-profile figure.

as shapeless but also to see that a meaning read into a field when it is a figure is not read in when the field is seen as ground."

Similar figure-ground reversals occur in the Indian-Eskimo drawing (Figure 3) and in the duck-rabbit drawing (Figure 4). When we view figures of this type, we usually demonstrate a visual sidedness, which is often connected with hand- and general body-sidedness. Right-handed and right-sighted individuals will most often see the Indian or the duck first, whereas left-handed and left-sighted people usually see the Eskimo and the rabbit first.

3. Indian-Eskimo figure.

4. Duck-rabbit figure.

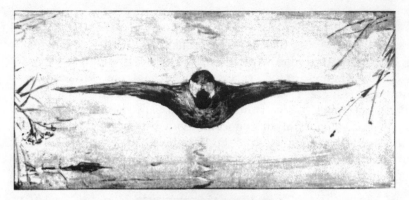

5. *Newell's duck-hound figure.*

6. *Newell's dog-cat figure.*

7. **Portrait of Madame Quilira.** *Reversible faces from a book called* Monstri, *about monsters of fact and fiction, published in Rome about* 1585.

Not all ambiguous figures can be seen from the same perspective. Reversible drawings such as the duck-hound and the dog-cat must be turned upside down (Figures 5 and 6). These examples were drawn by American illustrator Peter Newell, who published two volumes of reversible drawings in *Topsys & Turvys* around the turn of the century. Some reversible heads (for example, Figure 7) date back to the sixteenth century. Of recent vintage are the Scheherazade-prince figure and the Sherlock Holmes-Robin Hood figure that were drawn by the English artist Rex Whistler as part of a Shell Oil advertising campaign in the 1930s (Figures 8 and 9). These too must be turned upside down.

8. Left, Whistler's Scheherazade-prince figure.
9. Right, Whistler's Sherlock Holmes-Robin Hood figure.

Another type of ambiguous figure involves depth reversal rather than figure-ground reversal. This can be seen in the well-known Necker cube, named after the Swiss crystallographer L. A. Necker, who first described the figure in 1832 (Figure 10).

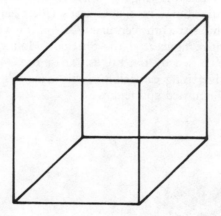

10. Necker's reversible cube.

Several factors contribute to this perplexing visual paradox. Unlike a perspective drawing of a cube, in which the front surface is drawn larger than the back surface, the Necker cube is drawn so that the front and back surfaces are of equal dimensions. This produces a retinal image which the brain can interpret in two ways, each corresponding to a projection of the cube viewed from a different position. Faced with the problem of which position the cube is in, the brain cannot settle on either, and continues to flip back and forth.

R. L. Gregory, a British psychologist and an expert on visual perception, has performed several interesting experiments using three-dimensional Necker cubes. In one experiment, a subject in a dark room held the skeleton cube, which had been given a luminescent coat of paint. The glowing outline of the figure reversed visually even though the subject *held* the cube in his hands and could *feel* one face of the cube in his hands while it *appeared* in another place.

In another experiment, which can be duplicated easily, a three-dimensional Necker cube is looked at in a dimly lighted room as an ordinary flashbulb is set off. The afterimage of the cube remains on the retina of the subject—and it too reverses. This signifies that the shifting is not a result of our eyes moving but that the brain is actively involved in the perception process as it attempts to work out which figure is there and in which direction it is placed.

Other depth-reversal figures include Schröder's staircase, devised by the German mathematician Ernst Schröder, and Mach's book, devised by the Austrian physicist Ernst Mach, as well as the well-

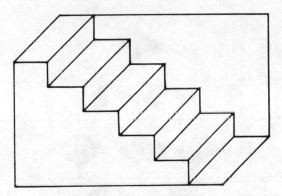

11. Schröder's famous reversible staircase is a classic ambiguous figure. At first it appears to be normal and right-side up, but upon continued viewing it will suddenly invert and appear to be upside down.

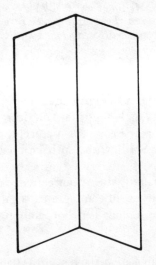

12. Mach's reversible book. The problem for the viewer is to determine if the book is open with its spine toward us or with its pages toward us.

known reversible cube pattern (Figures 11, 12, and 13). The reversibility in all three drawings is caused by the straightedge folds, all of which are ambiguous and can be read as either "in" or "out." Because of the symmetry of each drawing, no one interpretation is dominant. The ambiguity of the fold lines in these drawings is really an extension of the characteristics of the cube and its isometric projection into the plane as shown in Figure 14.

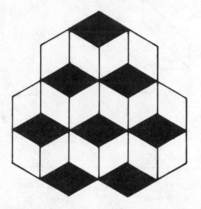

13. Reversible cube pattern. The reversal in this figure involves the direction of the cubes. At times the black sides appear to be the tops of cubes, and at other times the bottoms. At rare moments it is possible to see the figure as a plane crossed by black and white diamond shapes.

The Dutch artist M. C. Escher made use of the Necker cube in his lithograph *Belvedere* (Figure 22, in "M. C. Escher's Paradoxes"). Other artists including the American Bauhaus painter Josef Albers, the French op artist Victor Vasarely, and the contemporary American minimalist Sol Lewitt also have used ambiguous figures in their graphic work.

In his book *Inversions*, the American mathematician Scott Kim has combined elements of ambiguous figures, calligraphy, and word play to create a new type of ambiguous visi-verbal figure (Figures 15 and 16).

See also M. C. Escher's Paradoxes and Impossible Figures.

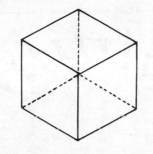

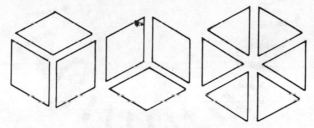

14. Isometric projection of a cube.

15. Upside-down, *by Scott Kim.*

16. Infinity, *by Scott Kim.*

THE PARADOX OF AMPHIBIUS

Imagine that a bowl of water which contains Amphibius, a tadpole, is filmed continuously for three weeks. At the end of the third week, the bowl contains a frog. Assuming that the camera functions perfectly at twenty-four frames per second, we can expect approximately 43.5 million frames. Now, suppose the frames are numbered 1 to 43,500,000 in the sequence in which they were filmed. It seems clear that frame 1 would show a tadpole but that frame 43,500,000 would not.

Yet, if this is so, then it follows logically that in the series there must be a frame showing a tadpole that is directly followed by a frame showing a frog. The validity of the logic is a result of applying the principle of the least number, a theorem of mathematical logic which states that for any given series 1 to n, if 1 has a certain predicate, or defining characteristic, and n does not, then there must be a "least number" (among the set of numbers that form the series) which does not have the predicate. In other words, there is a frame that shows a tadpole and, within one twenty-fourth of a second, the next frame shows a frog. Most people find the existence of such a frame to be counterintuitive, for how would a person go about identifying the picture in question?

The Amphibius tadpole-frog paradox was originally formulated by James Cargile, a professor of philosophy at the University of Virginia. Cargile's problem is really a variation of one of the oldest paradoxes of Western civilization. In its original formulation the argument dealt with the impossibility of making a heap by adding one seed at a time. It is from this version, which can be traced to the Greek philosophers of the school of Megara in the fourth century B.C., that the sorites paradox gets its traditional name, *sorites* being the ancient Greek word for "heap." Other variations of the paradox include arguments which show that there can be no such thing as a wealthy man or a bald man. In each variation, the essence of the logic is that there can be no borderline case that can be used to decide if something is a tadpole or a frog, a heap or not a heap, and so on.

Let us first consider one of the classical versions of the sorites paradox—that of the wealthy man—before we return to Cargile's tadpole-frog variation. In our version of paradox of the wealthy man, we begin with a poor man who asks a stranger for a penny. The beggar hopes that if he panhandles enough pennies he will be a wealthy man. The stranger points out to him that his goal is impossible. After all, if a man has just one penny he is not wealthy, and if he is given one more penny, he is still not wealthy. Once having accepted the principle that adding a single penny will not make the beggar a wealthy man and then applying this principle again and again, the beggar is forced to conclude that no matter how many pennies he receives, he will still not be a wealthy man.

Of course, one way to destroy the stranger's argument is to have trucks filled with pennies drive up and dump them in a "heap" at the beggar's feet. (The beggar couldn't do this, but some eccentric billionaire could.) This would be a pragmatic counterexample of the most dramatic sort. To a student of paradoxes, however, the point is to find the *logical* flaw in the stranger's reasoning, and this the pragmatic counterexample fails to do. The basic argument can be reduced to the following statements:

If a man has a penny, he is not a wealthy man.
If a man is not a wealthy man, then giving him one more penny will not make him a wealthy man.
Therefore, regardless of how many pennies you give a man, they will not make him a wealthy man.

The argument is valid from a strictly logical viewpoint; that is, if the premises are true, then by the rules of logic the conclusion must be true. We know for certain that the first premise is true—one penny does not make a man wealthy. Consequently, it seems sensible to suppose the problem lies in a false second premise. Yet, if we negate the second premise and say, "If a man is not wealthy, then giving him one more penny will make him a wealthy man," we are sure to conclude that this too is false, for it by necessity must assert that a very precise boundary line exists between being wealthy and being not wealthy. Our experience tells us that the word *wealthy* as we use it is a bit more vague than that. Yet, if both the second premise and its negation are false, then at least one of the fundamental laws of logic would appear to be on shaky ground.

Consider, for example, the three basic laws of thought upon which classical logic is built. The law or principle of identity states that if anything is p, then it is p. If I am a human, then I am a human; the law of identity is satisfied. The law of excluded middle says that anything is either p or not-p—either I am human or I am not human. Finally, there is the law of contradiction which holds that nothing can be both p and not-p; it cannot be the case that I am both human and not human.

It is obvious from the rules above that a statement p and its negation not-p cannot have the same truth value: if one is true, the other must be false. (This is the law of bivalence.) Yet, every variation of the paradox of the heap would have us believe that it is possible for both a statement and its negation to be false. Something must give. Some philosophers say that certain of the laws of classical logic (usually the law of excluded middle) should be discarded; others claim that it is our two-valued logic that is the problem; still others assert that the real problem is that the paradox is not articulated precisely enough to be handled by the methods of formal logic.

Many contemporary philosophers claim that there are formal logical solutions to the sorites paradox. Most of them believe that the paradox is deeply rooted in the ambiguities of the language used to express it. These commentators assert that the problem is caused by the words *wealthy* and *heap*. Such words are considered vague, rather than ambiguous, terms. Ambiguity arises when a word or expression can be interpreted in two or more ways. A vague term is one that does not provide a precise cutoff; that is, it does not tell us when someone passes from being not wealthy to being wealthy. If we consider these two characteristics as being opposite ends of a continuum, then somewhere between them we expect to find a dividing line. In fact, although such a borderline may exist, vague terms such as *wealthy* or *heap* do not allow us to identify the cutoff point—that is precisely what makes them vague.

Another significant aspect of the fallacious reasoning used in the paradox of the wealthy man relates to the very notion of significance. It is true that each additional penny does not provide the necessary borderline case to distinguish being not wealthy from being wealthy. However, taken together, the pennies do make a difference; and if there are enough of them, they do make a person wealthy. In other words, a series of insignificant changes can, when taken together, be quite significant.

This is clearly relevant to those variations of the paradox that involve quantifiable elements such as how many pennies make a man wealthy or how many seeds make a heap. But what happens if we are concerned instead with the acquisition of some characteristic or quality, as is the case in Cargile's tadpole-frog variation?

One possible approach to Cargile's variation is to claim that it is, in fact, quantifiable. For example, one could argue that at frame 1 Amphibius is 100 percent tadpole. Then, as each fraction of a second passes (and as each frame records Amphibius' development), the percentage of tadpoleness decreases. According to Cargile, "the fact remains that he [Amphibius] must eventually reach 0.0 percent and there must be some exact first picture where this is so. And that this final disappearance of tadpoleness from Amphibius takes place at an instant is just as surprising, and the determination of this instant is just as mysterious, as in the case of the property of being a tadpole."

According to Cargile, who classifies his own views as realistic, there is a moment at which Amphibius ceases to be a tadpole and at the next is a frog. It may be the case that we do not know which instant this is, and it may make no difference that we do not know, but logic requires that the instant must be. In a 1969 article, "The Sorites Paradox," Cargile claims:

> What is essential is that there will be one moment when Amphibius is a frog, such that, an instant before, he was not. . . . It is not being denied that, for the young tadpole Amphibius it will be a long time until he is a frog . . . growing can take lots of time. But acquiring properties does not. It is like reaching the top of a mountain. We can say that it took five hours to reach the top. And yet we can also say that at the end of four hours and 59 minutes of climbing we had not yet reached the top, and at the end of five hours, we had.

Cargile's paradox of Amphibius has a formal analogue in one of Zeno's paradoxes. Regardless of how close we might come to identifying the two frames in question, it would seem that we are doomed to fail, because it is possible—at least, in theory—to photograph an infinite number of instants between any two adjacent frames. Thus, the moment of becoming in which Amphibius changes from a tadpole to a frog must always slip between the cracks. As we shall see later, the paradox of Amphibius can be "resolved" by applying concepts from the theory of infinite sets, but it is difficult to diffuse the metaphysical problems created by the paradox.

See also The Infinite Hotel Paradox and Zeno's Paradoxes.

THE BARBER PARADOX

A certain village has among its inhabitants one and only one barber. He is a clean-shaven and well-respected man who shaves all and only the village men who do not shave themselves. These are the facts. The question is, "Who shaves the barber?"

At first, it seems plausible that the barber would shave himself. However, if he does, then he is violating the stipulation that he shaves all village men who do *not* shave themselves. Yet if he does not shave himself, then the barber is violating the stipulation that he shaves *all* village men who do not shave themselves. Who, then, shaves the village barber?

This paradox was first presented in 1918 by the British philosopher Bertrand Russell. If the paradox is reduced to its simplest terms, we find that we are dealing with two sets of village men: those who shave themselves and those who do not and, therefore, are shaved by the barber. The real question is to which group does the barber belong? In fact, the barber belongs to neither set because, as shown above, his existence would produce the contradictory conclusion that he shaves himself if and only if he does not. In fact, as the American philosopher Willard V. Quine has observed, the paradox itself can be considered a valid proof for the fact that the barber cannot exist: it appears to be a classic case of a *reductio ad absurdum*.

However, the matter is not so simple, for the paradox is exactly parallel in structure to another of Russell's paradoxes, that of the set of all sets that do not contain themselves as members. Russell introduced this earlier paradox in 1901, and it had a great impact on twentieth-century mathematical thought. Referring to the significance of the paradox, the German mathematician Gottlob Frege, the founder of modern mathematical logic, said, "Arithmetic trembles."

At the heart of Russell's paradox is the belief that for every description or property specified there is a corresponding set; that is, a set is constructed by stating a necessary and sufficient condition for belonging to it. Thus, if we specify the condition of being a satellite of the earth in the year 100 B.C., anything that exhibited these characteristics—for example, the moon—would be a member of the set of "satellites of the earth in 100 B.C." If we were to further specify the set of "man-made satellites of the earth in the year 100 B.C.," we would be dealing with a set that was empty; that is, one that had no members, but one that was nevertheless a set, the null set, as it is called.

Russell's antinomy is concerned with the self-membership of a set. Sets of some objects clearly are not members of themselves, for example, the set of the earth's satellites in 1980 is not a member of itself because it does not orbit the earth. Nor is the *set* of all recreational logic books a member of itself, for as the American logicians James Carney and Richard Scheer have noted, it has no pages, no text, no binding, and no price.

The fact that the sets of some objects do not contain themselves as members does not mean that there are no sets which are members of themselves. Consider, for instance, the set of all sets that have more than ten members. This would contain many sets including the following: the set of all artificial earth satellites in 1980, the set of all recreational logic books, as well as the set of all cats, the set of all dogs, the set of all birds, the set of all snakes, the set of all camels, the set of all puffins, and the set of all egrets, not to mention the set of all flowers, the set of all vegetables, the set of all trees, the set of all algae, and so on. Thus, it is quite clear that the set of all sets containing more than ten members has itself more than ten members and is therefore a member of itself. After all, if the set of all sets that have more than ten members was not a member of itself, then it would not be the set of *all* sets with more than ten members.

Now let us look again at those sets that are not members of themselves—the sets of artificial satellites, recreational logic books, etc. The question becomes, "Is the set of all sets that are not members of themselves a member of itself?" For convenience, let us call the set of all sets that are not members of themselves X. If we argue that X is a member of itself, then by definition it is not a member of itself for X contains only those sets that are not members of themselves. Similarly, if we argue that X is not a member of itself, then by definition it is a member of itself for X contains all those sets that are not members of themselves. Hence, X can neither be nor not be a member of itself; yet, clearly, because of the law of excluded middle, it must be one or the other. In ordinary language this means that the set of all sets that are not members of themselves is not a member of itself if and only if it is a member of itself. We are faced with a contradiction.

In his solution to the paradox of the set of all sets that are not members of themselves, Russell rejected the principle of abstraction. He concluded that the set of all sets that are not members of themselves is *not* a set. As Quine notes in his essay, "The Ways of Paradox":

> The principle [of abstraction] is not easily given up. The almost invariable way of specifying a [set] is by stating a necessary and sufficient condition for belonging to it. When we have stated such a condition, we feel that we have "given" the [set] and can scarcely make sense of there not being such a [set]. The [set] may be empty, yes; but how could there not be a [set] at all? What substance can be asked for it that the membership condition does not provide? Yet such exhortations avail us nothing in the face of the antinomy, which simply proves that principle untenable. It is a simple point of logic, once we look at it, that there is no [set], empty or otherwise, that has as members precisely the [sets] that are not members of themselves. It would have to have itself as a member if and only if it did not.

Russell argued that we must reject the notion that there is a set that corresponds to every predicate; that is, that for every assertion of a property or a characteristic there is necessarily a set whose members exhibit that property or characteristic. Russell regarded those predicates which give rise to contradictory consequences as meaningless in the sense that they did not produce a set. As Quine notes above, the mere attempt to define a set gives us mistaken support for its existence, whereas when we define a set all we are really doing is presupposing the *possibility* of its existence. Yet it is clear that the definition of a set, if it is to be a good definition, should satisfy the conditions for existence among which is the principle that these defining conditions should not be self-contradictory. Just as we cannot describe a figure as a "square circle" because "square" and "circle" are contradictory notions, so too we cannot describe a set in terms of contradictory characteristics.

Russell was able to remove the paradox by suggesting that the principle of abstraction be withheld in those situations where the membership condition mentions membership. This does, indeed, remove the paradox and allows the principle of abstraction to be used in those areas of mathematics that involve the concept of set in a secondary or tangential way. However, the effect of this restriction on general set theory was enormous. It took the use of subscripts to distinguish between different levels of language to make logicians comfortable with the restrictions on self-membership. As we shall see, Russell's solution to his own set paradox is similar in this respect to Alfred Tarski's solution to the liar paradox. Both solutions also force us to reject deeply and intuitively held notions, one of set and the other of truth.

There are other ways to remove the contradiction involved in the Russell set paradox, one of which involves the construction of a set theory based on a many-valued logic and not on our classical two-valued, true-or-false logic. In such a system, negation has a different meaning from its traditional one, and thus it is possible for a set to be both a member of itself and not a member of itself.

Russell's paradox of the set of all sets that are not members of themselves bears a strong resemblance to Kurt Grelling's paradox of heterologicality and to G. G. Berry's paradox of the least integer (see "The Heterological Paradox"). However, unlike these others, Russell's set paradox had a real influence on the development of mathematical thought and is still the subject of some debate. It is remarkable for its simplicity in that it involves only the notions of set and membership, whereas the other paradoxes involve complex and ambiguous language and are essentially semantic in nature.

See also THE HETEROLOGICAL PARADOX.

THE CROCODILE'S DILEMMA

A crocodile seized a human baby who had been playing on the banks of the Nile. The mother implored the crocodile to return her child. "Well," said the crocodile, "if you can predict accurately what I will do, I will return the child. However, if you guess wrong, I will eat it for my lunch."

"Oh, you will devour my baby!" cried the distraught mother.

"Now," said the wily crocodile, "I cannot return your baby, for if I do return it, I shall make you speak falsely and I warned you that if you spoke falsely I would devour it."

"Quite the contrary," said the clever mother, "you cannot devour my baby, for if you do devour it, you will make me speak the truth and you promised me that if I spoke truly, you would return my baby. I know you are an honorable crocodile and one who will keep his word."

Who is the logical winner of this argument? What, logically speaking, will happen next?

The oldest treatment of this dilemma is traced to Diogenes Laërtius, the ancient Greek biographer who lived in the third century A.D., although other references indicate that it may go back to the Sophist philosophers of the fifth century B.C. The dilemma is related, in its history and its structure, to the lawyers' paradox; it is really an elaborate variation of the liar paradox.

The question seems not to be who is the logical winner of the argument but rather if there can be *any* winner, for there appears to be no way out of the dilemma.

It seems that from the crocodile's viewpoint it doesn't matter if the mother speaks truly or falsely. After all, if she speaks truly the

17. Crocodile, drawn by Harry Furniss, from Lewis Carroll's Sylvie and Bruno.

crocodile cannot return the child without destroying the truth of the mother's statement. Similarly, if the mother has spoken falsely, the crocodile still cannot return the child, because the mother has not fulfilled the agreement.

From the mother's viewpoint it doesn't matter if she has spoken truly or falsely. If the mother has spoken truly, then by the terms of the agreement the crocodile must return the baby. Then, too, the mother can be said to have spoken falsely only after the child has been returned. Therefore, whether the mother speaks, truly or falsely, the child must be returned.

To understand the logical inconsistencies buried in the mother's and the crocodile's arguments, it is helpful to summarize their views. The crocodile's argument can be expressed as follows:

> If the mother accurately predicts what I will do, then I will return the baby.
> If I return the baby, then the mother has not accurately predicted what I will do.
> Therefore, I will not return the baby.

The mother's views can be expressed in the following form:

If I accurately predict what the crocodile will do, then my
baby will be returned to me.

If my baby is not returned (that is, devoured), then I predicted accurately what the crocodile will do.

Therefore, the baby will be returned to me.

Consider the two premises of the crocodile's argument. As the
crocodile states in the first premise, he returns the baby if and only
if the mother accurately predicts what he will do. However, according to the second premise, if he does return the baby, then the
mother's prediction is false. But how can this be, if based on the
first premise the baby can be returned if and only if the mother
predicts accurately? The point is that it *can't* be, for as we have
just demonstrated, assuming that the agreement can be kept leads to
validly deduced contradictory conclusions. A similar analysis can be
made of the mother's argument.

Lewis Carroll offered the following pragmatic solution to the
crocodile's dilemma in *Symbolic Logic*, Part II: "Whatever the
Crocodile does, he *breaks* his word. Thus, if he devours the Baby,
he makes her (the Mother) speak truly, and so *breaks* his word; and
if he restores it (the Baby) he makes her speak falsely, and so
breaks his word. His sense of honour being thus hopeless of satis-
faction, we cannot doubt that he would act in accordance with his
second ruling passion, his love of Babies!"

Carroll suggested that his readers try to work out the problem if
the mother's first statement had been, "You will return the Baby."
In this case, if the crocodile returns the baby, then it has kept its
word. If it devours the baby, then the mother has spoken falsely,
and the crocodile still has kept the bargain. Thus, Carroll reasoned
that, "whatever the Crocodile does, he *keeps* his word. Hence his
sense of honour is entirely satisfied, whatever he does, so that, again,
his only guide is his *second* ruling passion—and the result to the Baby
would, I fear, be much the same as before."

The American philosopher and logician William Warren Bartley
III, who discovered and edited the lost second volume of Carroll's
Symbolic Logic, suggests that Carroll may have been pulling the
wool over his readers' eyes by offering a "solution" that is really
just another analysis of the problem. As Bartley notes, "The proof
of the spoof is in the putting." Many logicians of Carroll's day

believed the crocodile's dilemma and related paradoxes were unsolvable. As we shall see later, in our discussions of the lawyers' paradox and the liar paradox, there are several contemporary approaches to the resolution of this type of problem.

See also THE LAWYERS' PARADOX and THE LIAR PARADOX.

M. C. ESCHER'S PARADOXES

Among the best-known works of the Dutch graphic artist M. C. Escher is the lithograph *Drawing Hands* (1948). It represents a pair of hands, each of which is busily drawing the other and both of which are illustrated on a piece of drawing paper which is itself tacked onto a drawing board. The lithograph contains several paradoxical elements, the most obvious of which is the vicious circularity of the self-reference created by each hand's drawing of the other. However, there is also an ancient artistic contradiction represented here and that is the conflict between the two-dimensionality of a figurative drawing and the three-dimensionality of the world it represents. In this sense, *Drawing Hands* may be interpreted as a metadrawing, one which restates this conflict as well as the famous dictum, "Every artist draws himself."

In *Drawing Hands* and in many other works, Escher is overtly telling his viewers that all drawing is a form of illusion. However, with Escher this deception is executed with such visual logic that a viewer cannot escape the contradictory effects it produces. Many of Escher's prints are like formally constructed logical paradoxes. They seem to be built from true premises (images) by means of good reasoning (composition) and yet produce contradictory conclusions (impossible worlds). Escher's interest in the paradoxical took many directions, but none was more important than his use of periodic drawings called "tessellations."

A plane tessellation involves the division of a two-dimensional surface into a periodic checkered or mosaic pattern. Escher considered this activity "the richest source of inspiration that I have ever tapped." His interest in the idea that a planar surface could be divided in such a way that it consisted entirely of congruent figures

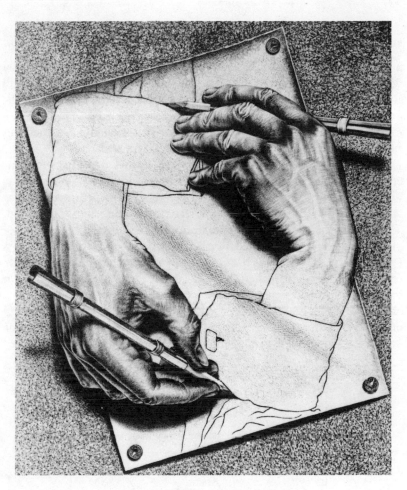

18. Drawing Hands, *by M. C. Escher.*

with no gaps between them can be traced to his university days at the School of Architecture and Ornamental Design in Haarlem, Netherlands.

Escher made an attempt at a regular periodic space-division drawing in 1926, shortly after a brief visit to the Alhambra, the Moorish citadel near Granada, Spain. However, it was not until 1936, after an extended visit to Granada, that Escher became totally absorbed by the principles and techniques of tessellation. It was during this second trip that Escher, with the help of his wife, made numerous copies of the Moorish tessellations which decorated the walls of the Alhambra. The Moorish patterns, however, were all abstract because Islam prohibited figurative art in public or religious places; nevertheless, these designs fascinated Escher, who saw in them an enormous potential for figurative tessellations, something no Moorish artist or anyone else had ever attempted.

Without the benefit of mathematical knowledge, Escher proceeded to "invent" the basic rules of tessellating a plane surface, which also turned out to involve the general principles of crystallography, the study of crystal structures and their formation. These principles are easily understood if we consider the example of a plane surface covered with congruent equilateral triangles (Figure 19). Imagine that a duplicate of this pattern has been made on a piece of tracing paper. Now, if the tracing paper is placed on top of the original paper in such a way that the two designs coincide, a crystallographer would say the two designs are "mapped onto" each other. If the tracing paper is slid left or right or up or down, the two designs will soon coincide again. This mapping is ac-

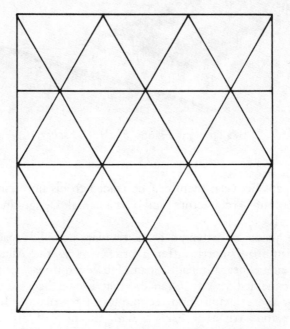

19. Plane surface of congruent equilateral triangles.

20. Day and Night, *by M. C. Escher.*

complished by the principle of translation. If the tracing paper is rotated 60 degrees around the apex of any of the triangles, the designs will also coincide but this time by the principle of rotation. Finally, if the tracing paper is picked up and turned upside down, the designs are mapped onto each other by the principle of reflection. These three principles can be seen throughout Escher's tessellations.

Escher's fascination with tessellations was reinforced by his growing interest in Gestalt psychology, which was gaining in significance throughout the European intellectual community of the late 1930s. It was through the experimental work of the Dane Edgar Rubin, the German Kurt Koffka, and other Gestalt psychologists that Escher learned to transform his images from two- to three-dimensional representations and to vary the brightness contrast so as to make the viewer perceive certain areas as figure or as ground.

The combination of tessellation and Gestalt psychology provides the basis for much of Escher's work. Among the most perfect of his woodcuts is *Day and Night* (1938), shown in Figure 20. At the bottom center of the picture we see a simple checkered pattern of diamond-shaped fields. As we move upward toward the center of

the picture, these squares are transformed in a few steps into a flat
pattern of black and white birds and then into a pattern of three-
dimensionally represented birds. Only the central pattern of black
and white birds is made of equivalent figures, and it is an example
of a tessellation developed solely by means of the principle of translation. The movement of each flock of birds, like the change from
field to bird, involves a transformation of ground into figure. These
transformations involve a subtle use of brightness contrast and shading which force certain figure-and-ground perceptions on the
viewer. Escher first learned of these techniques in the experimental

21. Circle Limit IV, *by M. C. Escher.*

work of the American psychologist Molly R. Harrower, a student of Koffka.

The central area of Escher's woodcut *Circle Limit IV* (1960) contains a more complex tessellation wherein angels and devils alternate as figure and ground (Figure 21). As we move outward from the center in any direction, the figures continually get smaller and smaller, but they always maintain their space-filling characteristics. This reduction technique involves a special type of non-Euclidean geometry called "hyperbolic geometry," which was invented by the French mathematician Henri Poincaré. Poincaré developed his new geometry using a model in which an infinite flat plane was shown to be within a large finite circle. Escher's discovery of an illustration of Poincaré's model led to the development of Escher's series of *Circle Limit* woodcuts.

Circle Limit IV is especially powerful because it reflects Escher's beliefs in the duality of nature and in the pursuit of infinity. In Bruno Ernst's book, *The Magic Mirror of M. C. Escher*, the artist is quoted as having written:

> Good cannot exist without evil, and if one accepts the notion of God then, on the other hand, one must postulate a devil likewise. This is balance. This duality is my life. Yet I am told that this cannot be so. People promptly start waxing abstruse over this sort of thing, and pretty soon I can't follow them any further. Yet it is really very simple: white and black, day and night—the graphic artist lives on these.

Late in his career Escher began to use impossible figures in his graphic work. He succeeded in creating mind-boggling worlds of contradiction such as the one portrayed in his 1958 lithograph *Belvedere* (Figure 22). The Italianate building certainly does live up to its name with the extraordinary views it provides. The top floor of the belvedere appears to be oriented in the direction of the young lady's view, whereas the bottom floor is oriented in the direction of the lord's view. The view from each floor is perfectly plausible, but only when taken separately; the views cannot all exist together in a three-dimensional structure, as Escher would have us believe.

There are other contradictory elements in the belvedere. For example, the ladder, although perfectly straight and properly angled, appears at the bottom to be inside the belvedere but, contrary to

22. Belvedere, *by M. C. Escher.*

expectations, appears to be on the outside of the structure at the top. Then, too, there is the matter of the columns that connect the two stories of the building. The columns on the far right and far left are normal; but the others connect front to back or back to front in impossible ways.

Escher provides some excellent clues as to the nature of this remarkable building. Sitting on a bench at the bottom of the belvedere, a young man holds in his hands an impossible cuboid. On the floor lies yet another clue, a drawing of a reversible figure, the Necker cube, with two points of intersection circled. The Necker cube is an ambiguous figure that involves depth reversal, producing two views of the cube with each view oriented in a different direction (see "Ambiguous Figures"). The circled intersections correspond to those points at which the directionality of the lines forming the edges of the Necker cube have been altered to force an impossible view on the observer. The construction of impossible cuboids from the Necker cube is shown in Figure 23.

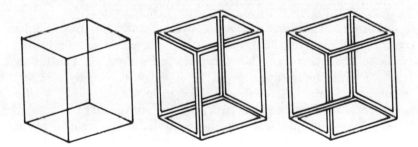

23. *Necker cubes.*

Similarly, Escher's *Belvedere* consists of two separate drawings joined together by a single paradoxical perspective. You can demonstrate this for yourself by taking a white sheet of paper and placing it so that it covers the top half of the belvedere. Be sure to place the lower edge of the paper on the lower foot of the man higher on the ladder. You will notice that the man lower on the ladder is clearly inside the belvedere and that the columns no longer make impossible connections. Conversely, you will see that the man on the top of the ladder is clearly outside the belvedere, if you look at the top half of the drawing while covering the bottom half.

Escher's 1960 lithograph *Ascending and Descending* shows another paradoxical world, one in which two opposing lines of hooded, monklike figures simultaneously ascend and descend a rectangular system of stairs (Figure 24). On first viewing this drawing, one has the sense of being allowed to peek at the most sacred ritual of some ancient monastic order as its members contemplate the ineffable object of their devotion.

Upon closer examination, the viewer discovers that the ascending monks *always* appear to be ascending, while the descending monks *always* appear to be descending. The more closely one examines the drawing, the stronger the illusion becomes; it persists despite the fact that we know that the rectangular staircase structure is closed. What accounts for this stunning paradoxical visual effect wherein one can always ascend or descend without getting higher or lower?

The staircase structure of *Ascending and Descending* is based closely on an impossible staircase originally presented by L. S. Penrose and Roger Penrose, a British geneticist and his mathematician son, in the *British Journal of Psychology* in 1958 (Figure 25). The illusion of the Penrose impossible staircase can be explained if the structure is shown schematically sliced. If you follow level 1 from its highest vantage at the upper right, you will see that it reappears at the base of the stairway structure. Likewise, level 2 reappears at the bottom of the structure, just above level 1.

Quite obviously, the *levels* do not really lie in a horizontal plane, but rather move upward spirally; however, the steps of the stairway *do* remain in a horizontal plane. In Escher's print, the other parts of the building including the window frames and columns actually spiral upward and the staircase itself remains horizontal. The whole building looks perfectly logical, but only from the front; such a building could not have a back and still stand. Escher's drawing also has some anamorphic properties. If you view it holding it horizontally, just below eye level, you will see that the structure appears to rise slightly from the page as do all anamorphic figures. The fact that the stairway itself is on one plane becomes more apparent when the picture is viewed in this way.

Escher pursued other paradoxical themes in his graphic work in-

24. Ascending and Descending, by M. C. Escher.

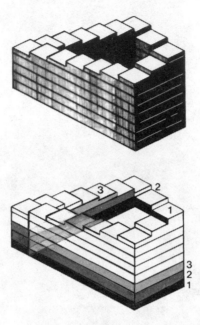

25. The Penrose impossible staircase.

cluding the representation of Möbius bands (Figure 85) and un-
usual and contradictory perspectives; yet, despite his remarkable
achievements in representing the paradoxical, Escher once wrote,
"If only you knew the things I have seen in the darkness of the
night . . . at times I have been nearly demented with a wretch-
edness at being unable to express these things in visual terms. In
comparison with these thoughts, every single print is a failure, and
reflects not even a fraction of what might have been."

See also AMBIGUOUS FIGURES, IMPOSSIBLE FIGURES, PERSPECTIVE
PARADOXES, and TOPOLOGICAL PARADOXES.

GEOMETRIC VANISHES

The simplest type of geometric vanish involves the loss of all or part of a line. Perhaps the oldest is the vanishing line paradox, shown in Figure 26. This figure presents a rectangle with seven vertical lines of equal length and a broken diagonal line which divides them.

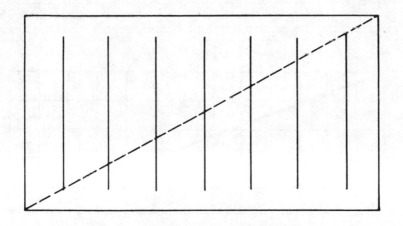

26. The vanishing line paradox, I.

If the rectangle is cut along the diagonal and the two pieces are placed together so that the bottom part is moved one segment to the left, suddenly one vertical line vanishes and there are only six lines left (Figure 27). Where did the missing line go?

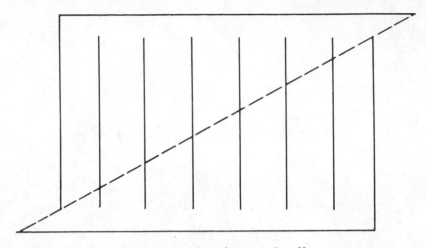

27. *The vanishing line paradox, II.*

A more sophisticated type of geometric vanish involves the apparent loss of area. Consider, for example, the arrangement of squares shown in Figure 28. The entire figure contains sixty-five smaller squares arranged to form a rectangle that is five units high by thirteen units wide.

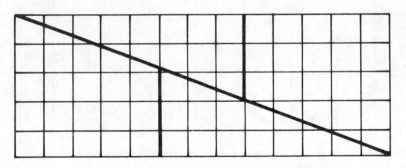

28. *The vanishing square paradox, I.*

Suppose we dissected the square and rearranged its parts to form the square shown in Figure 29. Nothing seems paradoxical until we examine the area of the new figure and find that it is an eight-unit-by-eight-unit square. Thus, it has an area of sixty-four units rather than sixty-five. Where did the missing unit go?

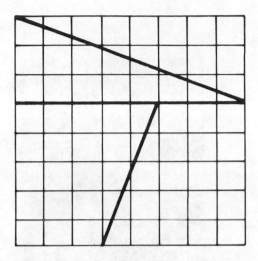

29. The vanishing square paradox, II.

All geometric vanishes involve a drawing which when cut into parts and rearranged produces in its new configuration a loss or gain in length or area. The cause of the vanishing line paradox is really quite simple: the lengths of the original lines are, in fact, redistributed so that each of the six new lines is slightly longer than each of the seven old lines. The difference is not very noticeable; however, the incremental difference in the length of each new line adds up to the exact length of the missing line.

The explanation for the decreased area paradox is somewhat different from that for the disappearing line paradox. On a practical level, the apparent loss or gain of area takes place as a result of the fit of the pieces along the diagonal in Figures 28 and 29. In fact, the edges do not coincide exactly but instead form a minute, almost unnoticeable parallelogram. A large and fairly careful construction of these figures does show the parallelogram. Vanishes with illustrations usually have deceptive lines; these and the irregularities of the edges caused by the cutting account for the mysterious gain or loss of area.

Area vanishes generally involve line segments whose lengths form a Fibonacci series; that is, a series in which each number is the sum of the two preceding numbers: 1, 1, 2, 3, 5, 8, 13, 21, 34, 55. . . . In the case of the square and the rectangle, the figures have sides of 5, 8, and 13, and are clearly part of a Fibonacci series. As Martin

30. The disappearing egg paradox.

Gardner points out in his book *Mathematics, Magic, and Mystery*, an outstanding characteristic of such a series is that if any number in it is squared, it will equal the product of the two numbers on each side, *plus or minus one*.

Among the best examples of geometric vanishes are two from the late nineteenth century. The disappearing egg paradox (Figure 30) is really a variation of the simple line vanish (Figures 26 and 27). In this case, each row of eggs is arranged in a diagonal fashion so that the cut would be horizontal rather than diagonal. The extra vertical cuts create four parts which when rearranged produce truly remarkable visual effects. The parts can be arranged to form pictures that show six, seven, eight, ten, eleven, or twelve eggs! Figure 30 shows arrangements in which there appear to be eight and ten eggs.

The most famous of all vanishing paradoxes is Sam Loyd's "Get Off the Earth Puzzle" (Figure 31). Loyd, an American puzzlemaker at the turn of the century, ingeniously changed the puzzle from a horizontal line to a circle, thereby producing a vanish that involves only two parts but that produces startling appearances and disappearances.

31. "Get Off the Earth Puzzle," I.

When the earth is positioned on the rectangle so that the arrow points to the N.E. pole, you will be able to count thirteen Chinese warriors. But when the earth is rotated so that the arrow points to the N.W. pole, there are only twelve Chinese warriors (Figure 32).

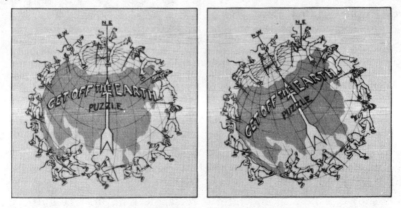

32. "Get Off the Earth Puzzle," II.

One of the most interesting contemporary vanishes was created by Paul Curry, an American mathematician and magician, who

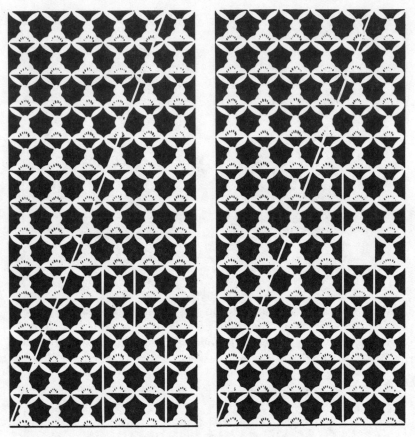

33. The disappearing rabbit paradox.

combined elements of the area vanish and the line vanish to create the disappearing rabbit paradox. In the original six-by-thirteen-unit rectangle, there are seventy-eight squares, each containing the silhouette of one rabbit (Figure 33, left).

When the rectangle is rearranged after cutting it apart along the lines shown, a new six-by-thirteen rectangle is formed (Figure 33, right). But this new one has only seventy-seven rabbits and one hole. Needless to say, there is only one place the rabbit could have gone.

See also AMBIGUOUS FIGURES and VISUAL ILLUSIONS.

THE GRUE-BLEEN PARADOX

Let us assume that the term *grue* is applied to an object if when observed before a certain time (*t*) it is green and when observed after that certain time it is blue. Similarly, an object that is blue before time *t* and changes to green thereafter is said to be *bleen*. For convenience, let us consider as time *t* midnight of the last day of the year 2000. If we buy a widget in 1984 and it is green but, at the first moment of January 1, 2001, it turns blue, then it is a grue widget. On the other hand, if the widget we bought in 1984 was blue at the time and changed to green at the stroke of the new year 2001, then it is a bleen widget.

But what of an emerald we buy in 1984 that we observe at the time of purchase to be green? It would certainly be fair to say that such an object would be a confirming instance that adds support to the generalization "All emeralds are green." However, consider the fact that we are observing the emerald's color before the start of the year 2001. This means that the observation that the emerald is green also adds support to the generalization that "All emeralds are grue"; for in order for something to be grue, it has to be green at all times before midnight of December 31, 2000. Inasmuch as all emeralds observed to date have been green and all such observations have been before time *t*, then there is no escaping the fact that both generalizations must be considered as equally confirmed.

Assuming we buy an emerald in 1984 and that it is indeed green at the time, what can we logically expect come the year 2001? Common sense will tell you to expect a green emerald, but logicians are still entitled to ask why is it more likely that the emeralds observed after time *t* will continue to be green rather than blue? Or, as the philosophers put it, why is the predicate "green" more projectable (more likely to be the same in the future as now) than the predicate "grue"?

The American logician Nelson Goodman first proposed this paradox in an article written in 1946 for *The Journal of Philosophy* and later expanded it in his book *Fact, Fiction, and Forecast,* published in 1955. Goodman's paradox resulted from a consideration of the German logician Carl Hempel's raven paradox. The two are clearly related, for both are problems of inductive logic, specifically, in the theory of confirmation which studies how we formulate and support our scientific hypotheses or generalizations.

In deductive logic one can say with certainty that a conclusion is validly drawn from its premises, and if the premises are true then the conclusion *must* be true. This is not the case in inductive logic, particularly in enumerative induction, which is concerned with support for generalizations of the "All emeralds are green" type. Here, the best we can say is that there is a great deal of support for the generalization. The counterintuitive result of the grue-bleen paradox is that a single confirming instance appears to support inconsistent generalizations in a perfectly logical way.

Goodman himself has suggested that the problem turns on the projectability of predicates of the type used in inductive logic. Goodman distinguishes his new problem of induction from the old one formulated by the Scottish philosopher David Hume. Hume's question was how do we justify the inductive inferences that we make? For example, how do we justify the prediction that all emeralds we observe in the future will be green on the basis of our past observations of a limited number of emeralds? Hume's answer was that we justify our inductive inferences by "custom and habit." Goodman claims that his paradox is concerned with how we distinguish between predicates like "green," which appear to be projectable into the future, and those like "grue," which do not. Goodman's tentative solution seems to be that certain predicates are more entrenched than others; that is, they are more acceptable than others because of "custom and habit."

Most of the debate concerning Goodman's paradox has focused on the question of whether or not the words *grue* and *bleen* are positional. *Grue* and *bleen* do appear, at first, to change their defining characteristics at an arbitrarily specified moment in time. Yet, as Goodman himself points out, this view depends somewhat on which terms we consider as having come first. Thus, if we as

English speakers think of some set of things as green or blue, then we think of these predicates as projectable because as English speakers we are used to thinking so. However, a person who speaks a different language, one in which *grue* and *bleen* are words that are projectable by custom and habit, then it is *green* and *blue* that are positional.

A related approach to solving the grue-bleen paradox attempts to show that certain predicates such as "green" are projectable because they are time-independent, whereas others such as "grue" are time-dependent and, hence, not projectable. Consider, for example, this thought experiment suggested by the Israeli philosopher Yael Cohen of the Hebrew University of Jerusalem:

> An anthropologist [who] is a native speaker of Greenese studies a tribe speaking Gruese. He has no special problems in acquiring the everyday vocabulary of the tribal language. However, when he discovers that everything he calls 'green' the tribesmen call 'grue' he suddenly recollects that once he heard some weird story about this predicate and the year 2000 from [a philosopher friend]. He therefore asks the tribesmen: "Do you believe that these emeralds in the tribal coffer will be grue after the year 2000?" Their answer is "Yes!" So far, our anthropologist has no reason to suspect that 'grue' may differ in meaning from 'green.' However, one sunny day, in a jungle clearing, while the tribesmen are seated around the emeralds from their tribal coffer, the wise anthropologist asks them to perform the following thought-experiment. "Imagine," he says to the tribesmen, "that today everyone is overcomed by a deep sleep, not to awaken until long after the year 2000. Of course, on awaking, the first thing you do is to check your emerald treasure. Suppose that your sensations are exactly the same as those you have right now. Would the emeralds which you would then observe be grue?" Only the more clever tribesmen succeed in fathoming the anthropologist's question but they answer with no hesitation: "Surely not! The emeralds would be bleen." (Because of the definition of 'grue' and 'bleen' the speakers of Gruese must answer in this way.) It is then that it dawns on the anthropologist that the word 'grue' has a different role in the tribal language from the word 'green' in his own. At this juncture he also realizes that the hypothesis "All emeralds are grue" is incompatible with the hypothesis "All emeralds are green." Moreover, the surprised anthropologist discovers that the thought-experiment he performed with the tribe

provides him with a criterion for preferring the hypothesis "All emeralds are green." Anyone observing a green (grue) emerald today, when asked to imagine that he has slept for an *unknown* period, such that on awaking all his sensations are exactly the same as those he has now while observing the emerald, will determine without hesitation (irrespective of his native language) that the emerald in the thought-experiment is green. But without any further temporal information he would not be able to decide whether the emerald is grue or not. Thus the experiment has shown that the predicate 'grue' is time dependent, while the predicate 'green' is not.

As Cohen notes, if there is, in principle, no way to establish today that there is a difference in meaning between *green* and *grue*, then there can be no way to establish this difference—which the paradox asserts exists today—at any moment after the time *t*. The definition of *grue* provided in the problem makes *grue* different from *green* only if we assume that it is possible to distinguish differences in the meaning of the two words and not just differences in their signs—in the physical marks or sounds that we use to express these words in writing and speech. According to Cohen, determining the time-dependency distinction between *grue* and *green* is sufficient to diffuse the paradox.

Many philosophers reject the time-dependency approach as a satisfactory way to resolve the grue-bleen paradox. For example, according to the British philosopher A. J. Ayer, Goodman's paradox really involves the conjunction of two contrary statements—"Some Xs are Ys" and "Some Xs are not Ys"—masquerading as a universal generalization. Furthermore, Ayer argues that Goodman's grue-bleen paradox can be re-created without reference to a specific time *t*. Ayer does this by introducing the term *greemin*, which he says applies to any member of a group of objects all of which are green, with one exception that is blue. In such a situation, any observation of a green emerald is a confirming instance of the hypothesis that "All emeralds are green" and, as long as there are still other emeralds to observe, it also is a confirming instance of the generalization that "All emeralds are greemin." Although these hypotheses are obviously incompatible, Ayer asserts that regardless of how comfortable we are with certain predicates, it is still possible for the same evidence to provide equal support for two incompatible hypotheses.

Some philosophers have tried to resolve the grue-bleen paradox by suggesting that there exists within us innate generalization classes by which we establish which predicates are projectable and which are not. For instance, the Israeli philosopher Nathan Stemmer argues that behavior research has shown that members of a species exhibit a specific type of instinctive behavior wherein they generalize about future cases based on a few past observations.

Stemmer claims that evolution, with its process of natural selection, makes such behavior beneficial to the survival of the species, since if the instinct for generalization were not beneficial, it would have disappeared. Thus, according to proponents of the innate theory of projectable predicates, it is evolution which provides us with the "custom and habit" needed to justify certain inductive inferences and to reject others.

Goodman and others have objected to this view. They claim that evolution cannot be used to justify our preference for the projectability of the predicates "blue" and "green" over those of "grue" and "bleen" because the set of grue objects before time t can be said to have played the same role in evolution as the set of green objects.

Another approach to the grue-bleen paradox was offered by Lin Chao-tien, who argued that it was possible to avoid the resulting contradictions by using a three-valued logic, one which involves truth (confirmation of the generalization), falsity (disconfirmation of the generalization), and neutrality (neither confirmation nor disconfirmation of the generalization). Under such a system, the grue-bleen paradox cannot be generated.

There have been numerous other attempts to solve the grue-bleen paradox, but no one has succeeded in satisfactorily explaining why we should find the predicate "green" more projectable than "grue." If the volume of literature it has generated is a genuine indication of its significance, then it may be that the grue-bleen paradox has the characteristics of a truly important problem for the philosophy of science.

See also THE RAVEN PARADOX and TIME PARADOXES.

THE HETEROLOGICAL PARADOX

A professor of English, while lecturing to a class of freshmen, enumerated the several types of adjective: true adjectives, participial adjectives, predicate adjectives, demonstrative adjectives, and so on. When he finished the traditional list, he paused for a second and then added, "And, of course, there are autological and heterological adjectives which I am sure you know nothing about, since I made them up just last night. Nevertheless, they are quite legitimate as types, I assure you. Autological adjectives are those which are true of themselves. The adjective *small* is small and, hence, is autological. Likewise, the adjective *polysyllabic* is autological, because it applies to itself. Words such as *long* and *monosyllabic* are heterological. These words are *not true* of themselves; that is, they do not possess the properties they express."

As soon as he stopped speaking, a hand went up at the back of the room and a student said, "Professor, excuse me, but I'm a little confused. Would you consider the adjective *heterological* to be heterological or autological?"

"Hmmm. Why, heterological—yes, heterological."

"But then," replied the student, "if the word *heterological* is heterological, then it applies to itself, and if that's so, then by definition it is autological."

"Well, yes, yes—that's right, autological."

"But if you decide that the word *heterological* is autological, then the adjective by definition is true of itself. However, that would make the word heterological and not autological. After all, whatever the word *heterological* is true of must be heterological. Isn't that so?"

"Why, yes and no," sputtered the bewildered professor.

What is the correct classification of the adjective *heterological?* Is it heterological or autological?

In 1908 Kurt Grelling, a German mathematician, posed the original version of this paradox, which he called the "paradox of heterologicality." Since its first presentation, it has captured the attention of many philosophers including the Englishmen Bertrand Russell and F. P. Ramsey and the American Willard V. Quine. The paradox is similar in structure to Russell's barber paradox and to his set paradox.

The forces of contradiction at work in the paradox can be brought more sharply into focus by reducing the problem to its most essential elements. Consider, for example, two sets of adjectives, those that are "self-descriptive" and those that are "non-self-descriptive." To which set would the adjective *non-self-descriptive* belong? If you say "non-self-descriptive," then the adjective is, in fact, self-descriptive; yet, on the other hand, if you say that the adjective is "self-descriptive," it becomes non-self-descriptive. Even simpler is the version in which there are two sets of adjectival phrases, those "true-of-self" and those "not-true-of-self." To which set would the phrase *not-true-of-self* belong? Quite obviously, the phrase *not-true-of-self* cannot be both true and not true of itself, but this is what this form of the paradox would have us believe.

Some commentators have dismissed this problem as essentially a semantic one. For instance, Ramsey in his analysis maintains that "the contradiction is simply due to an ambiguity in the word 'meaning' and has no relevance to mathematics whatsoever." Others, such as the British philosopher Joshua C. Gregory, maintain that the problem really involves a confusion between a word, its sign, and its meaning. Gregory believes that the word *heterological* may be mythical, having mistakenly been given some credibility by the fact that it is possible that some meanings do apply to their verbal signs—for example, the meaning of the word *short* applies to the physical brevity of the word.

The Pakistani philosopher Intisar ul-Haque claims that in order for a word to be considered heterological or autological, it is necessary for it to designate some property other than that of heterologicality or autologicality. Heterologicality (or autologicality) is a dependent property; that is, a property whose existence logically requires the existence of some other property by which we may measure its heterologicality (or autologicality).

The accepted solution to Grelling's paradox lies in an examination of two fundamental notions relating to our concepts of set and language. Russell provided an insight into the solution of this paradox in his simple theory of types. According to Russell, sets are described as being arranged in a hierarchy of types. For example, cats are members or elements of the set of all cats; this is a first-order set. The set of all cats can be an element of a second-order set such as the set of all vertebrates. However, according to Russell and later mathematicians and logicians, the set of all cats cannot be a member of itself; that is, not without producing the kind of contradictions examined in the paradox. Similarly, there can be no adjective *not-true-of-self* which is a member of the set of all adjectives "not-true-of-self." Such an adjective, like Russell's barber, cannot exist.

Yet on an ordinary language level, the adjectival phrases *true-of-self* and *not-true-of-self* would seem to apply in the situation described. The paradox is difficult to dismiss unless one also makes a distinction between language and metalanguage. Just as there is a hierarchy of sets, one can also pose a hierarchy of metastatements. Descriptive statements about the real world—"All cats are animals" and "My cat is black"—are considered examples of object language, the lowest level of language in the hierarchy. Statements about these statements—such as "The statement 'My cat is not black' is false" or "The statement 'My cat is black' is true"—cannot occur in object language, but only in first-level metalanguage; that is, in language about language. Similarly, first-order metalanguage can be discussed only in second-order metalanguage, and so on, ad infinitum.

For convenience, mathematicians and logicians usually add subscripts to such expressions. As Quine notes:

> Whereas 'long' and 'short' are adjectives that can meaningfully be applied to themselves, falsely in the one case and truly in the other, on the other hand 'true$_0$ of self' and 'not true$_0$ of self' are adjectival phrases that cannot be applied to themselves meaningfully at all, truly or falsely. Therefore to question "Is 'true$_0$ of self' true$_1$ of itself?" the answer is no; the adjectival phrase 'true$_0$ of itself' is meaningless of itself rather than true$_1$ of itself.

Thus, the paradox can be avoided if we make certain that when we make a statement about the truth or falsity of another statement, we always do so in a metastatement with a higher subscript than that of the statement about which we are commenting. Any statement that violates this principle is considered not true or false, but ungrammatical and meaningless; more precisely, its truth value is undecidable and unverifiable.

The paradox of the least integer, which is closely related to Grelling's heterological paradox, was also first presented in 1908. Russell published and analyzed the paradox of the least integer, which had been formulated by a British librarian named G. G. Berry. According to the paradox, the ordinary English name of any integer contains a certain number of syllables; for example, "twenty-one" contains three syllables and "two thousand five hundred and thirty-three" contains ten syllables. The number of syllables in these names tends to increase as the integers grow larger, and only a finite number of such names can be constructed, for a given number of syllables. It follows then that the names of some integers must contain nineteen syllables and among them there must be a *least* integer; that is, there must be a definite integer that is named by the expression "the least integer not nameable in fewer than nineteen syllables."

According to Bertrand Russell that number is, in fact, 111,777 ("one/ hun/dred/ and/ e/le/ven/ thou/sand/ se/ven/ hun/dred/ and/ se/ven/ty/ se/ven"). Of course, there are other numbers (such as 211,777) nameable in nineteen syllables, but there is only one number that is the *least* integer not nameable in fewer than nineteen syllables.

But think again. The expression "the least integer not nameable in fewer than nineteen syllables" is itself a name for the number in question, and it names the integer in eighteen syllables! Thus, we are faced with the contradiction that the least integer not nameable in fewer than nineteen syllables is, in fact, nameable in fewer than nineteen syllables.

Russell maintained that the solution to Berry's least integer paradox, like the solution to Grelling's heterological paradox, could be achieved by distinguishing between different orders of language; in this case, different orders of names for integers. As with Grelling's paradox, Berry's paradox also contains a considerable amount of ambiguity. The expression under discussion would seem to mean something like "the least integer not nameable in fewer than nineteen syllables using the ordinary English counting system." But what exactly is the ordinary English counting system? Russell argued that 111,777 was the least integer in question based on the counting expression presented above. But the same number can be expressed in ordinary English in fewer than nineteen syllables; for example, "one/ hun/dred/ e/le/ven/ thou/sand/ se/ven/ hun/ dred/ se/ven/ty/ se/ven," which contains seventeen syllables. Then, too, we might use the ordinary English expression "Three/ thou/ sand/ and/ twen/ty/ one/ mul/ti/plied/ by/ thir/ty/ se/ven," which contains fifteen syllables.

Obviously, the expression "the least integer not nameable in fewer than nineteen syllables" is ambiguous and does not refer to any particular integer unless the method for formulating the ordinary English counting expression has been specified. Nevertheless, even if there exists a precise, unambiguous system for creating English counting expressions, we are still dealing with two orders of naming expressions. According to Russell and others, the word *nameable* remains systematically ambiguous unless we mention the corresponding order of language with which we are dealing. Consequently, Russell argued that the nineteen-syllable expression should be rephrased as "the least integer not nameable in fewer than nineteen syllables of the order n." Now this expression itself, when considered a name, belongs not to the order n but to the order $n + 1$, for its function is to describe the counting expressions that comprise the first level of language.

Thus, as with Grelling's heterological paradox and Russell's own barber paradox, there is a hierarchy of language functions operating in Berry's least integer paradox, and to resolve it we must distinguish names of different orders. The contradiction disappears once we have specified the level of language being used, for it is perfectly consistent and logical that two or more names from different language levels may denote the same number in different numbers of syllables.

See also THE BARBER PARADOX and THE LIAR PARADOX.

IMPOSSIBLE FIGURES

An impossible figure is a drawing that represents an object that cannot exist in the real world. Among the most famous of these figures is the impossible trident shown in Figure 34.

The problem for the viewer is to determine the status of the middle prong. If you look to the right of the figure, the three prongs all appear to be on the same plane; that is, they seem to share the same depth relationship. Yet, if we look to the left of the figure, the middle prong appears to drop to a plane lower than that of the two outer prongs. Where exactly is the middle prong located?

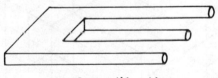

34. Impossible trident.

Although in reality the middle prong cannot be in both places at once, apparently a drawing can be made using ambiguous lines so that the contradiction can be visualized. In fact, as with most impossible figures, the impossible trident works by means of a "false" connection; that is, a connection which can be made in the two-dimensional space of a drawing but which cannot be made in the three-dimensional world we live in. According to R. L. Gregory, a British expert on visual perception, such figures strictly speaking cannot be "perceived" because the brain cannot formulate an acceptable perceptual hypothesis for them (Figures 35 and 36).

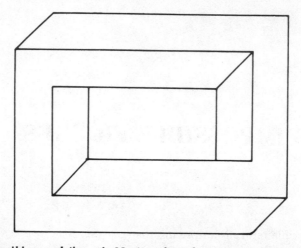

35. *Impossible quadrilateral. Notice that this illusion works by means of false connections. The corners of the "quadrilateral" connect impossibly in the same way as do the angles of the Penrose impossible triangle in Figure 37.*

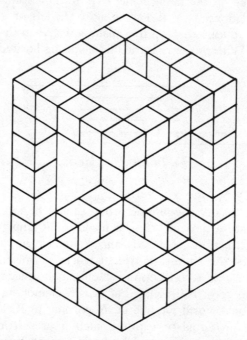

36. *Impossible cuboid. Here the impossible connections are made by the central rib of the cuboid which appears to connect the front to the back.*

Another well-known impossible figure is the Penrose impossible triangle (Figure 37), designed by L. S. Penrose, a British geneticist, and his son Roger, a mathematician and physicist (the designers also of the staircase in Figure 25, above, in "M. C. Escher's Paradoxes). The impossible tribar, as it is more accurately called, presents many of the same perceptual problems to the viewer as the trident in Figure 34. At first viewing, the object seems to resemble an equilateral triangle, but upon closer examination we realize that each angle is a normal right angle and that the three have been put together in a spatial arrangement that is impossible in the real world. Each corner of the object presents a different angle of viewing to the observer. If added up, the angles of this "triangle" would total 270 degrees.

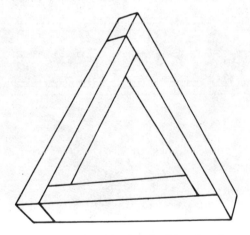

37. The Penrose impossible triangle.

The Dutch graphic artist M. C. Escher knew of the Penrose figure and put it to great effect in his 1961 lithograph *Waterfall* (Figure 38). If we begin by looking at the top of the left-hand tower, we see water falling and striking a wheel, thereby causing the wheel to turn. The fallen water then flows through a brick channel, where it appears always to be moving downward and away from us. Finally, the water ends up where we began—at the top of the left-hand tower—only to drop once again on the wheel below.

38. Waterfall, *by M. C. Escher.*

39. Basic structure of Escher's Waterfall.

The basic composition of *Waterfall* involves three impossible triangles linked together (Figure 39). The details of Escher's drawing, especially the water-flow lines and the diminishing brick walls of the channel structure, help to create the illusion that the water is constantly receding from us. In fact, there are really no three-dimensional angles here, just as there are none in the impossible triangle. The triangular aqueduct structures are also not shown in perspective; notice, for example, that the aqueduct channel that is farthest away is not smaller than those closer to us. Escher distracts us with the strong use of perspective in the house structure and in the landscape, especially the polyhedra on the tower tops.

Escher's interest in impossible figures can be seen in other works. As we noted in our discussion, above, he used Necker's impossible cuboid in his 1958 lithograph *Belvedere* (Figure 22) and the Penroses' impossible staircase in his well-known 1960 lithograph *Ascending and Descending* (Figure 24).

Implicit in the definition of an impossible figure is the idea that

40. Three-dimensional model of an impossible triangle, I.

the object represented, such as the tribar, cannot exist in a three-dimensional world. But then how are we supposed to account for the unretouched photograph (Figure 40) of a three-dimensional object that appears to be consistent in all respects to the impossible Penrose triangle?

The image you see is of an actual three-dimensional object, and it does appear to have the same configuration as the Penrose triangle. However, this is true of the image but not of the object, as we can see by the view shown of it in Figure 41.

The fact is that from one precise perspective this three-dimensional object creates the same retinal image as the Penrose figure. As Gregory notes in his essay "The Confounded Eye":

> We *assume*, incorrectly, that the two ends of the object [in Figure 40] lie at the same distance, and are in physical contact. In fact, they lie at different distances and are only *optically* in contact. Having accepted this single false assumption—which is difficult or impossible to resist—we at once generate a paradoxical perception; for the other features, such as the perspectives of the corners, are incompatible with the sides lying in a plane. What is happening is that a three-dimensional object is being "described" perceptually with an hypothesis assuming it to be on a two-dimensional plane except for the corners, which receive three-dimensional treatment, incompatible with the overall two-dimensional account. This generates the perceptual paradox which resists our intellectual understanding.

41. Three-dimensional model of an impossible triangle, II.

Other three-dimensional models of the impossible triangle can be constructed. According to the American mathematician Scott Kim, who wrote an extraordinary article in *Hypergraphics*, a 1978 collection of articles on complex visualizations, these include an embossed model and a curved model (Figures 42 and 43). When viewed from the correct angles, these three-dimensional models will also project a retinal image that is consistent with the Penrose drawing in Figure 37.

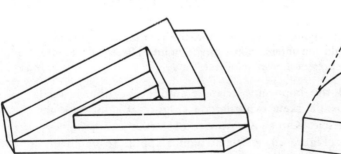 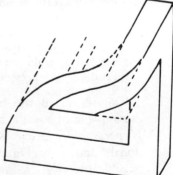

42. Left, embossed model of an impossible triangle.
43. Right, curved model of an impossible triangle.

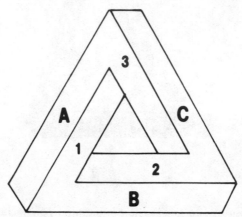

44. Impossibility proof for a three-dimensional model of the Penrose impossible triangle.

That such a three-dimensional triangle consistent in all respects with the image projected by the Penrose drawing is impossible can be demonstrated by mapping its faces as seen in Figure 44. The three visible faces have been labeled *A*, *B*, and *C*. Face *A* meets face *B* at edge 1; face *B* meets face *C* at edge 2; and face *C* meets face *A* at edge 3.

As Kim succinctly notes:

> No two of the planes containing any of the visible faces may be coplanar without the model going flat, hence they are all distinct. But three distinct non-parallel planes always intersect in a single point (assuming they lie in the same 3-space). Furthermore, each of the lines determined as the intersection of two of the planes must pass through this point. In fact, we can see that the lines containing edges 1, 2, 3, do not intersect in a single point. Therefore, [Figure 44] does not represent a possible object.

Kim translated the impossible triangle into a four-dimensional illusion—the impossible skew quadrilateral (Figure 45). In the same *Hypergraphics* article, Kim shows how to construct a three-dimensional "drawing" (Figure 46) of what would appear to be an impossible object to a four-dimensional person. (Apparently, Roger Penrose himself had built a model of such a figure some twenty years before Kim rediscovered it.)

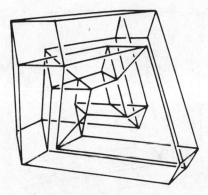

45. The impossible skew quadrilateral: a four-dimensional illusion.

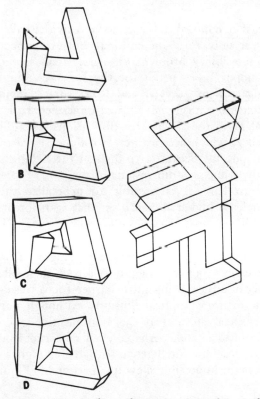

46. Plans for constructing a three-dimensional model of the impossible skew quadrilateral.

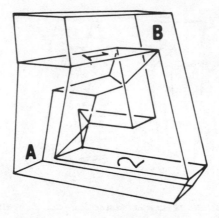

47. *Impossibility proof for the impossible skew quadrilateral.*

Of course, it is impossible for us to perceive visually the illusion because we are only three-dimensional, but Kim succeeds in presenting an impossibility proof in Figure 47 that is precisely analogous to the impossibility proof for the Penrose triangle in Figure 44. According to Kim, faces *A* and *B* are three-dimensional faces, each of which lies entirely in a three-dimensional plane. Faces *A* and *B* do not lie in the same three-dimensional plane, but they do meet at 1 and 2, which are distinct two-dimensional planes. However, this is impossible because two distinct three-dimensional planes may meet only at one two-dimensional plane.

According to Kim, it is possible to generalize the impossible Penrose triangle to higher dimensions; that is, to create five-, six-, and higher dimensional illusions. However, not all impossible figures can be translated to different dimensions; among those that can be is the Penrose impossible staircase (Figure 25). Kim notes that while we may not be able to perceive these illusions, they have value because they bring into sharper focus three-dimensional space and the nature of optical illusions. Although our perception of four-dimensional space may be non-intuitive, we can nevertheless comprehend it and, perhaps, even construct computer programs to allow machine intelligence to perceive higher dimensional illusions such as the impossible skew quadrilateral in Figure 45.

See also AMBIGUOUS FIGURES, M. C. ESCHER'S PARADOXES, and PERSPECTIVE PARADOXES.

THE INFINITE HOTEL PARADOX

Imagine an ordinary hotel with a finite number of rooms, all of which are occupied by guests. When a stranger arrives early one morning asking for a room, the proprietor is forced to turn him away with the standard statement, "Sorry. No vacancies." There is a difficulty here, but there is no paradox.

Now imagine the grandest hotel of them all, the Infinite Hotel, in which there are an infinite number of rooms, each of which is occupied. Suppose the same traveler arrives at the registration desk asking for a room. "Sorry, we are all full," the proprietor says cheerfully, "but we can certainly give you a room." What does the proprietor intend to do to accommodate his new guest and to resolve his own contradictory statements?

Furthermore, imagine that later that very same day the impossible occurs again. This time, at noon, an endless stream of conventioneers arrives (presumably from a parallel universe), and the proprietor is faced with an infinite number of new guests who wish to check in. Being an astute businessman, the proprietor realizes that if he can accommodate all his new arrivals, he could make a fortune. What can he do?

These paradoxes were first posed in the 1920s by the German mathematician David Hilbert. To provide a room for the single guest, Hilbert suggested, the proprietor should move the guest who is occupying Room 1 into Room 2, then move the guest in Room 2 into Room 3, the one in Room 3 into Room 4, and so on, ad infinitum. The new guest is then taken by the bellboy to Room 1, which is now vacant as a result of the shifts. "That was relatively simple," beams the clever proprietor, who is happy that he had to move each guest only one room down the hall.

The proprietor's second problem appears to be much more complex. If he accommodates the infinite number of new guests one at a time as he did the first, he will fit all of them in; however, the old guests are sure to become disgruntled by being constantly moved to the next room. Hilbert proposed the following solution to the proprietor's problem: move the old guest in Room 1 into Room 2, move the old guest in Room 2 into Room 4, move the old guest in Room 3 into Room 6, move the one in Room 4 into Room 8, and so on, ad infinitum. These changes will put the infinite number of old guests into all the even-numbered rooms. The hotel proprietor can then check the infinite number of new guests into the odd-numbered rooms.

Hilbert's paradoxes are firmly rooted in Georg Cantor's theory of transfinite numbers. Cantor, another German mathematician, was the first to deal adequately with the paradoxes that infinite sets had created for mathematicians since ancient times. Cantor presented his theory in 1873, but many mathematicians of his day were openly hostile to it. His French contemporary Henri Poincaré, for example, called Cantor's work "a disease." The criticisms hurled at Cantor caused him great mental anguish. However, shortly before his death in 1918, mathematical opinion began to shift, and today Cantor's theory is universally viewed as the work of an extraordinary mathematical genius.

The problems of infinity that Cantor sought to resolve can be traced to ancient Greece, in particular to the paradoxes of Zeno of Elea. However, for our purposes it is preferable to begin with some of the insights into infinity that Galileo revealed in 1634 in his *Dialogues Concerning Two New Sciences*. Considering a problem similar to Hilbert's Infinite Hotel paradox, Galileo realized that the set of all positive integers (1, 2, 3, 4, . . .) is infinite, but he also discovered that the set of the squares of all positive integers is infinite also. Galileo proved this by demonstrating that there was a one-to-one correspondence between the items in both sets:

$$1 \quad 2 \quad 3 \quad 4 \ldots n \ldots$$
$$\updownarrow \quad \updownarrow \quad \updownarrow \quad \updownarrow \quad \updownarrow$$
$$1 \quad 4 \quad 9 \quad 16 \ldots n^2 \ldots$$

Thus, it seems logical to conclude that there is an equal quantity of numbers in each set, for there is one and only one number in each set which corresponds to a unique number in the other set. Similarly, it can be demonstrated that the set of all even positive integers or the set of all odd positive integers is infinite and has a one-to-one correspondence with the set of *all* positive integers:

$$
\begin{array}{ccccc}
1 & 2 & 3 & 4\ldots n\ldots \\
\updownarrow & \updownarrow & \updownarrow & \updownarrow & \updownarrow \\
2 & 4 & 6 & 8\ldots 2n\ldots
\end{array}
$$

$$
\begin{array}{ccccc}
1 & 2 & 3 & 4\ldots n\ldots \\
\updownarrow & \updownarrow & \updownarrow & \updownarrow & \updownarrow \\
1 & 3 & 5 & 7\ldots 2n-1\ldots
\end{array}
$$

These facts startle us, for we expect the set of even positive integers to be only a *part* of the set of all positive integers. Similarly, we expect that the set of all odd positive integers to be only part of the set of all positive integers. In the course of his investigations into the nature of infinity, Galileo pondered the question of whether or not we should consider the set of all positive integers as larger than the set of the squares of the positive integers. He concluded that the relations of "equality," "greater than," or "less than" are applicable to finite sets but not to infinite ones, such as those we have been discussing. Galileo's insight into the one-to-one correspondence exhibited by such infinite sets proved to be more significant than even he realized, for it was this exact principle which Cantor, over three centuries later, used in his resolution to the paradoxes of the infinite sets.

Instead of rejecting the relations of "equality," "greater than," and "less than" when dealing with infinite sets, Cantor took the one-to-one correspondence principle and made it part of his definition of an infinite set. According to Cantor, an infinite set is one which can be shown to be in one-to-one correspondence with a part, or proper subset, of itself.

Galileo was unable to reach this conclusion because he was unwilling to give up these Euclidean principles: the whole is always equal to the sum of its parts and, therefore, the whole is always greater than any of its parts. Euclid's principles are true for finite sets, but, as Cantor proved, they are not true for infinite sets. In fact, it is the inappropriate application of these Euclidean principles to infinite sets that causes the paradoxes. Thus, applying Cantor's definition of an infinite set to Hilbert's Infinite Hotel paradox, the contradictions vanish.

Cantor used a system of subscripts to generate a hierarchy of transfinite numbers to represent the numbers of elements in infinite sets. The transfinite number that represents the quantity of integers in the set of all positive integers he called "aleph-null," symbolized as $\aleph_0$. Any set of numbers that enjoys a one-to-one correspondence with the set of all positive integers—for example, the set of all even positive integers—is itself an $\aleph_0$ set.

Cantor used a method of proof, called the "diagonal method," to demonstrate that there is a set with a greater infinite number of elements than the $\aleph_0$ set. To begin with, consider a finite set that contains only two members, x and y. Mathematicians show such a set by placing brackets around its members—$\{x, y\}$. Now, every set —even the null set that has no members—has subsets. A subset of a specified set such as $\{x, y\}$ is a set in which all its members are also members of the specified set. If every element of set A is an element of set B, then A is a subset of B.

The set of $\{x, y\}$ has four subsets: $\{x, y\}, \{x\}, \{y\}$, and $\{\phi\}$. Notice that any specified set is a subset of itself and that the null set $\{\phi\}$ is a subset of every set, including itself. Although $\{x, y\}$ is a subset of $\{x, y\}$, the subsets $\{x\}, \{y\}$, and $\{\phi\}$ are said to be *proper* subsets. A set A is a proper subset of set B if all the elements of set A are members of set B, but all elements of B are not members of set A; that is, there is at least one element of set B which is not a member of set A. We can determine how many subsets a specified set has by calculating the value of 2^n, where n is the number of elements in the specified set. Thus, as we have just seen, a set with two members has 2^2, or four, subsets, one with three elements would have 2^3, or eight, subsets, and so on. The null set, which has no members, has 2^0, or one, subset: itself.

As Martin Gardner notes in a March 1966 *Scientific American* article dealing with the problems of the hierarchy of infinities, we

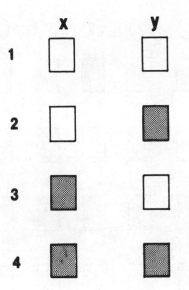

48. Subsets of a set of two elements.

can represent the subsets of the set x, y by using an array like the one shown in Figure 48. Here, an item x or y is represented by a white card if it is a member of a subset and by a gray card if it is not.

The same approach can be taken to determine if the subsets of the $\aleph_0$ set can be placed in one-to-one correspondence with the set of positive integers; that is, do the subsets of the $\aleph_0$ set form another $\aleph_0$ set? First, we assume that this is so and then create an infinite square array, such as the one shown in Figure 49. As Gardner notes in his explanation of Cantor's diagonal method:

> Symbolize each subset with a row of cards, as before, only now each row continues endlessly to the right. Imagine these infinite rows listed in any order whatever and numbered 1, 2, 3, . . . from the top down. If we continue forming such rows, will the list eventually catch all the subsets? No—because there is an infinite number of ways to produce a subset that cannot be on the list. The simplest way is to consider the diagonal set of cards indicated by the arrow and then suppose every card along this diagonal is turned over (that is, every face-down card is turned up, every face-up card is turned down). The new diagonal set cannot be the first subset because its first card differs from the first card of sub-

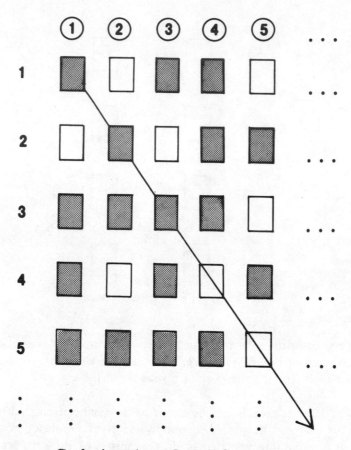

49. Gardner's version of Cantor's diagonal proof.

set 1. It cannot be the second subset because its second card differs from the second card of subset 2. In general it cannot be the *n*th subset because its *n*th card differs from the *n*th card of subset *n*. Since we have produced a subset that cannot be on the list, even when the list is infinite, we are forced to conclude that the original assumption is false. The set of all subsets of an aleph-null set is a set with the cardinal number 2 raised to the power of aleph-null. This proof shows that such a set cannot be matched one to one with the counting integers. It is a higher aleph, an "uncountable" infinity.

Thus, Cantor proved that there were other infinite sets of greater magnitude than that represented by the aleph-null designation. These he labeled with the transfinite cardinals $\aleph_1$ (aleph-one), $\aleph_2$ (aleph-two), $\aleph_3$ (aleph-three), and so on. The cardinality of a set is simply a measure of its size; that is, the number of elements it contains. For example, given that set $A = (x, y, z)$, then the cardinality of set A is said to be 3 and is written as $n(A) = 3$. If set $B = (x, x', y, y', z, z')$, then its cardinality is $n(B) = 6$. To say that set B is greater than set A simply means that the cardinality of B is greater than the cardinality of A.

Similarly, Cantor's system of transfinite numbers provides a way to compare the cardinality of infinite sets of differing magnitudes. Cantor proved that, as with finite sets, an infinite set such as $\aleph_0$ has more than $\aleph_0$ proper subsets; in fact, it has $\aleph_1$ proper subsets. Then, too, an infinite set with the cardinality $\aleph_1$ also has more than $\aleph_1$ proper subsets, leading to an infinite set with a cardinality of $\aleph_2$, and so on. By this method Cantor showed that there are more transfinite cardinals than there are counting numbers.

Cantor also proved that there was one set, consisting of the decimal fractions between 0 and 1, which was definitely larger than the aleph-null set but whose appropriate aleph-number he could not determine. This transfinite number he called C, for the power of the continuum. The continuum referred to the infinite set of points on any given line segment.

Cantor spent several years trying to prove that C was really equal to $\aleph_1$ but failed. Cantor's belief became known as the "continuum hypothesis," and it was not until 1938 that the Austrian-American mathematician Kurt Gödel proved that if we assume Cantor's continuum hypothesis to be true, set theory remained free of any contradictions. However, some twenty-five years later, another American mathematician Paul Cohen showed that if we assume Cantor's continuum hypothesis to be false, set theory also remains free of any contradictions. In other words, both statements about the continuum hypothesis, although clearly contradictions, are consistent with the axioms of set theory. The truth value of Cantor's continuum hypothesis is, in fact, undecidable.

Cantor's theory of transfinite numbers has produced several seemingly paradoxical results. Consider, for example, the fact that Cantorian proofs can be constructed to show that two lines of any length—for example, an infinitely long line and one that was one millionth of an inch long—would both have the same number of points and that a line a millionth of an inch long has the same number of points as there are in the entire universe.

Even the simplest arithmetical tasks such as addition and subtraction can produce paradoxical results when they involve infinite sets. For instance, recall the set of all positive integers which Cantor designated $\aleph_0$. We know that the set of all even positive integers is also $\aleph_0$ and so is the set of all odd positive integers. This means that $\aleph_0 + \aleph_0 = \aleph_0$; that is, $2\aleph_0 = \aleph_0$. Then, too, consider the set of all positive integers and the set of all positive integers beginning with 10. According to the theory of transfinite numbers, then $\aleph_0 - 10 = \aleph_0$.

This brings us to a final related paradox of infinity called the "Tristram Shandy paradox," after the eponymous hero of Laurence Sterne's novel of 1760. Tristram Shandy spent two years writing his autobiography and at the end of that period all he had recorded were the events of the first two days of his life. Shandy concluded that his autobiographical efforts were hopeless if he continued at the rate of recording one day each year. After all, as each year passed, Shandy would be certain to fall further behind. However, as Bertrand Russell noted, this is true only if we assume Shandy to be mortal. If we assume that Shandy will live forever, then it is quite possible for him to complete his life story. If he continues to record one day's events each year, he will achieve his goal at some time, for when dealing with an infinite amount of time there are as many days as there are years.

While such results play havoc with our intuitive understanding of finite numbers, they are acceptable—indeed, accurate—results in Cantor's theory of transfinite numbers. As American mathematician Morris Kline notes in his book *Mathematics in Western Culture:*

> Puzzles and paradoxes have been so much to the fore that the reader may regard the theory of infinite numbers as a mathematical *divertissement*. This is far from the correct evaluation. We should see rather how exact thinking has been applied to the shadow of one of the vaguest and most intangible intuitions. In rendering precise the notion of quantity as applied to infinite sets of objects,

Cantor disposed of reams of philosophic disputes which had taken place from Aristotle's time right up to modern times.

See also ZENO'S PARADOXES.

THE LAWYERS' PARADOX

The ancient Greek philosopher Protagoras was said to have taught the law to a poor student named Euathlus on the condition that Euathlus would repay Protagoras as soon as the student had won his first case. After completing his legal and rhetorical studies, Euathlus put aside his desire to practice law and decided instead to pursue a career in politics. Protagoras grew tired of waiting for Euathlus to pay the agreed fee and finally approached his former student and asked for payment. Euathlus rebuffed Protagoras, arguing that he owed Protagoras nothing, for, under the terms of the original agreement, Euathlus claimed that he was only required to pay *after* he had won his first case and that this had not yet happened. Protagoras, angered by his former student's position, sued Euathlus for his fee.

In the courtroom, both Protagoras and Euathlus argued their own cases with impeccable logic. Protagoras argued that if Euathlus lost the case, then he would have to obey the court and repay Protagoras. On the other hand, reasoned Protagoras, if Euathlus won, then he would have won his first case and, therefore, owed Protagoras the fee under the terms of the original agreement. In either case, Protagoras argued that his former student must pay the fee.

Euathlus' argument was equally reasonable and persuasive. He maintained that if he won the case, then the court would have ruled in his favor and agreed that he did not have to pay Protagoras. Euathlus further reasoned that if he lost the case, then he did not have to repay Protagoras either, because he still would not have won his first case.

Whose reasoning is correct? How would you expect the judge to rule?

The oldest reference to this dilemma can be found in Cicero's *Academica*, although it is generally attributed to the Stoic philosophers of ancient Greece. There are two major aspects to consider. The first is the logical problem of having two seemingly sound arguments that lead to completely contradictory conclusions. The second problem is that of the actual court ruling and what is required by law.

The logical problem in the lawyers' paradox is really another variation of the liar paradox. As in the case of the crocodile's dilemma, also a version of the liar paradox in the next chapter, one modern approach to the problem is to declare that, given the circumstances, the contract is an impossible one to fulfill. Precisely because the arguments by Protagoras and Euathlus are perfectly reasoned and validly lead to contradictory conclusions, it is obvious that the premises are inconsistent. However, as we shall see in the following section dealing with the liar paradox, there are other ways to deal with the lawyers' paradox including a metalinguistic approach and the use of a three-valued logic. Even so, the semantic and legal ambiguities of the lawyers' paradox make it difficult to resolve the problem in a purely formal, logical—and still satisfactory—way. In fact, it is these very ambiguities which make the lawyers' paradox such an intellectually interesting problem.

In order to understand which premises are the cause of the logical difficulty, it is necessary to distinguish between the terms of the original agreement and the claim of Protagoras' suit. The agreement says that Euathlus must pay Protagoras if and only if Euathlus has won his first case. The suit says merely that if Protagoras wins, then Euathlus must pay him the money. Protagoras' argument may be expressed thus:

> If I win the suit, then Euathlus must pay me the money.
> If I don't win the suit, then Euathlus has won his first case.
> If Euathlus has won his first case, then he must pay me the money.
> Therefore, Euathlus must pay me the money.

Euathlus' counterargument, on the other hand, can be reduced as follows:

> If Protagoras does not win the suit, then I do not have to pay
> him the money.
> If Protagoras wins his suit, then I have not won my first case.
> If I have not won my first case, then I do not have to pay Pro-
> tagoras the money.
> Therefore, I do not have to pay Protagoras the money.

Since Euathlus is defending himself in the case, the problem seems to rest in the third premise of Protagoras' argument and in the second premise of Euathlus' argument. Taken separately and in the context of their appropriate arguments, each premise seems quite reasonable. Yet taken together, these two premises merely indicate that Euathlus owes Protagoras the money if and only if he has won a case, which is equivalent to the original agreement. Thus, in order for these premises to be acceptable, one must presuppose the agreement has been kept, which is precisely what is impossible. Assuming the agreement has been kept means that the premises of the arguments must be inconsistent, and anything can be deduced validly from inconsistent premises.

Some commentators have argued that the problem rests in an ambiguity in the expression "the first case that Euathlus wins," which they say really means the first court case that Euathlus wins as a lawyer; that is, by defending or prosecuting someone. In Protagoras' argument a different meaning is implied, for Euathlus is involved, at least initially, only as the accused. Thus, the second premise of Protagoras' argument could not be said to deductively entail or guarantee the validity of the conclusion. This argument has little merit for, regardless of the wording of the original agreement, we can so modify the terms that they do indeed produce the con- tradiction described above provided that Euathlus defends himself.

In fact, according to proponents of the impossible-contract solu- tion, Euathlus is wise to defend himself because in so doing he achieves the best possible outcome for himself. It is true that he could engage another lawyer to defend him and still be assured that he would not have to pay Protagoras. After all, if Euathlus chooses not to defend himself, then he has never really acted as a lawyer and has not won his first case; consequently, he would not be required to pay Protagoras on the basis of the original agreement or on the basis of the suit.

Yet, by defending himself, Euathlus, though he makes the problem much more interesting, also manages to void the entire agreement by making it impossible to fulfill. On the other hand, had Euathlus not defended himself and taken up a law practice later, it would be possible for Protagoras to use the original agreement, which would still be binding, as the basis for another—and sure to be more successful—suit. By serving as his own counselor, Euathlus saves himself some potential problems, or so it would seem.

Several critics of the impossible-contract solution argue that while such a solution may be acceptable for the crocodile's dilemma, it does not adequately deal with the situation created by Protagoras' and Euathlus' arguments. The American philosopher W. K. Goossens and the German philosopher Wolfgang Lenzen have both noted that there is an additional ambiguity in the problem, one which relates to the nature of the court's ruling. A court ruling is concerned only with the past, and until the court rules in the case of Protagoras' suit, then Euathlus is still clearly living within the terms of the original agreement. Consequently, the court must deny Protagoras' suit.

However, the court's ruling functions in two ways: it settles Protagoras' suit and it also affects the original agreement, for it now means that Euathlus has won a case and is obligated to pay Protagoras. But note that this is *after* the verdict, *before* the verdict Euathlus had no obligation to pay Protagoras. There is a temporal as well as a logical meaning implied in the premise that Euathlus must pay if and only if he has won his first case. It is the distinction between these two meanings that must be clarified if we are to find an acceptable solution to the problem.

Proponents of this approach argue that once the verdict has been handed down, then Protagoras can ask Euathlus for payment on the basis of the original agreement. If Euathlus refuses to pay, then Protagoras can sue him again. Only this time Protagoras is almost certain to win, since now Euathlus has won his first case and has fulfilled the terms of the original agreement. If Euathlus agrees to pay, then it is interesting to note that at no time, either before or after the verdict, had he violated the agreement!

Goossens provides this helpful analogy in his analysis of the paradox:

Suppose X brings suit against Y for Z over some past contract, and the suit is denied. Does it follow that Y does not then legally owe Z to X? Not at all! Suppose X makes a written (and legal) bet over Z with Y that the suit will be denied. It is denied, so now Y does owe Z to X. The court ruled that Y did not owe Z to X, but as a result of the ruling Y owes Z to X. There is no contradiction.

Two aspects of the ruling have to be distinguished—the content of the ruling and the ruling as an in-the-world event. The content of the ruling in no way considers the consequences of it as an in-the-world event. The content of the ruling is based on the state of the world prior to the ruling. If you like, here the ruling is over a past contract. The bet itself—another contract—in no way affects the court's ruling, even if the court knew of it. The court ruling in no way overrides the bet. X could bring suit for Z on the basis of the previous denial that Y owed Z to X.

The case of Euathlus and Protagoras is just a special case of the above situation, with the twist that the two contracts are the same! It so happens that the ruling of the court as an in-the-world event is relevant to the conditions of the contract. Nevertheless, this consequence in no way affects the ruling itself.

As Goossens notes, according to this solution if Euathlus defends himself and loses, then Protagoras wins his case and gets the money, whereas if Euathlus uses another lawyer he continues to avoid payment until he wins his first case. Of course, in reality the court's decision is final (at least somewhere there is a final court ruling); and, in practice, the court could put aside one or more of the terms of the original contract on the grounds that they conflict with other legally relevant factors. For example, the court could decide in Protagoras' favor on the basis that the agreement clearly implied the intent on the part of Euathlus to practice law, and, by not doing so, he violated the original agreement. On the other hand, the court could also rule in Euathlus' favor that the contract is not binding. In either case, protests from the relevant party would do no good in the face of the court's power to make a definitive decision.

See also THE CROCODILE'S DILEMMA and THE LIAR PARADOX.

THE LIAR PARADOX

The most ancient and most important of all logical paradoxes is that of the liar. It is generally attributed to the Greek philosopher Eubulides of the school of Megara, which flourished in the sixth century B.C. The original formulation of the paradox required the liar to answer the question "Do you lie when you say you are lying?" If the liar responds "I am lying," then clearly he is not lying, for if a liar says he is a liar and he *is* a liar, then he speaks the truth. On the other hand, if the liar says "I am not lying," then it is true that he is lying, and, consequently, he *is* lying.

Another well-known formulation of the paradox involves Epimenides the Cretan, who says "All Cretans are liars." The problem then is to determine the truth of Epimenides' comment. A reference to this paradox appears in St. Paul's epistle to Titus (1:12), wherein he writes "One of themselves, even a prophet of their own, said, The Cretians are always liars. . . ." Paul's formulation, however, seems to miss the point, and contains ambiguities which make it impossible to generate the paradox.

Among the tidiest of the ancient formulations is the one called the *pseudomenon*, which simply asserts "I am lying." Other later variations include the statement "This sentence is not true," and the well-known calling-card version created by the French mathematician P. E. B. Jourdain in 1913. On one side of the card is the sentence "The statement on the other side of this card is true" and on the other side of the card is the statement "The statement on the other side of this card is false."

All the well-formulated variations have one thing in common: they force us to draw contradictory conclusions about the truth value of each statement. The question is, how do we go about diffusing this paradox?

The paradox of the liar has produced many commentaries by philosophers, scientists, and mathematicians from ancient times to the present. Its importance in the ancient world is evidenced by the number of serious thinkers who commented on it. Aristotle treated the problem on several occasions, and, as we shall see, his analysis of the paradox became the standard for more than a thousand years. The paradox was also treated by other ancients, including Aulus Gellius, Chrysippus, Seneca, and Cicero. One ancient logician, Philetas of Cos, supposedly died prematurely from frustration caused by his inability to solve the problem.

In his *De sophisticis elenchis*, a treatise on logical fallacies, Aristotle discussed the paradox of the liar in conjunction with another logical and moral problem, that of the perjurer. According to Aristotle, the problem of the perjurer is this: is it possible for the same person to be simultaneously a keeper of his oath and a breaker of his oath? For instance, suppose that a person swears that he will break his oath. Later, this same person swears that he will do something, but then breaks his oath and refuses to do it. Therefore, it would seem possible that the man, in fact, had kept his oath and had broken it at the same time. Aristotle maintains that this is an example of the fallacy of *secundum quid et simpliciter* and says, "For he who swears that he will break his oath keeps his oath in breaking that oath only, but he does not keep his oath." In other words, the man satisfies his oath only with respect to his first oath; that is, that he will break his oath. With respect to the second oath, the man is a perjurer.

In the same passage Aristotle proceeds to make an analogy between the resolution of the perjurer problem and the solution to the liar paradox, saying merely that the argument is similar to the problem of whether the same person can say something that is simultaneously true and false. It was left to other commentators to explain the liar paradox more fully along these lines. Later classical thinkers, including both Gellius and Cicero, followed Aristotle's lead. However, it was not until medieval times that the paradox of the liar was fully explicated according to Aristotle's analysis and shown, contrary to expectation, to be different in nature from that of the perjurer.

Consider, for example, the following twelfth-century version of the liar paradox, which appears to be exactly parallel in structure to Aristotle's problem of the perjurer. Suppose Socrates swears that he will speak only falsehoods to you, and later he comes to you and says "You are a stone." Then Socrates speaks the truth with respect to his oath that he will speak falsehoods; therefore, he speaks the truth. Likewise, Socrates can be said to lie because he speaks falsely. Therefore, the same person can both lie and speak the truth at the same time.

Many early medieval commentators continued to miss this point and to analyze the problem in terms of Aristotle's fallacy of *secundum quid et simpliciter;* however, in stating the problem, several of these formulations were clearly superior to earlier ones. For instance, Thomas Aquinas' version has the distinct advantage of using the present tense and thus avoiding time ambiguities. Aquinas says in his *De fallaciis,* "Likewise here, 'The Liar speaks the truth in saying that he speaks falsely. Therefore, he speaks the truth.' It does not follow. For to speak the truth is opposed to what it is to speak falsely, and conversely." Aquinas failed to extend his analysis to include the idea that the liar not only said "I speak falsely," but also said that that was *all* he said, which is the best way to generate the full force of the paradox.

Most thirteenth-century commentators also failed to formulate a completely rigorous statement of the problem, although a few did succeed. From the early thirteenth century to the late fifteenth century, an extraordinary tradition of *insolubilia*—problems that were thought to be unsolvable or at least solvable only with great difficulty—developed among medieval scholastics. Most *insolubilia* centered around the problem of the liar, and many of them took elaborate forms. Some of these problems had their sources in the classical sophisms of the Stoics (see "The Crocodile's Dilemma" and "The Lawyers' Paradox").

One of the most rigorously formulated variations of the liar paradox was discussed by the fourteenth-century Venetian philosopher Jean Buridan, who died about 1358. According to Buridan, Socrates makes a single statement, "What Plato says is false," and Plato, likewise, makes a single statement, "What Socrates says is true." As Buridan notes, if we say that what Plato says is false, then what Socrates says must be true. However, Socrates said that what Plato

says is false; and, therefore, what Socrates said must be false. Consequently, we must conclude that Socrates' statement is at the same
time both true and false.

Buridan resolves the paradox by claiming that there is an ambiguity in the meaning of the phrase "at the same time." Buridan
argued that every statement has a time associated with it, and if we
do not carefully specify the time intended, then contradictions
arise. For example, if we use time in a general indiscriminate sense,
then the statements "Socrates is dead" and "Socrates is alive" appear
to be contradictory. Yet, we know that it is quite possible for each
statement to be true or false, but only at different times. Thus,
"Socrates is dead" may be false at time t_1 but true at time t_2, and
"Socrates is alive" may be true at time t_1 but false at time t_2. According to Buridan, the liar paradox vanishes if one attaches appropriate times to the statements, "What Plato says is false" and "What
Socrates says is true," for it is quite possible for both statements to
be true at different times.

Another standard medieval solution to the liar paradox involved
the doctrine of *cassatio;* that is, to any person who asserts that he is
lying, the correct analysis is that he says nothing. Medieval proponents of this view argued that insoluble sentences of the liar type
really do not express propositions at all and, hence, cannot be
judged as true or false—they are meaningless. Such views were not
original to the medieval thinkers, although they were probably un-
aware of classical sources that expressed similar views.

The doctrine of *cassatio* may have originated in a brief comment
made by Aristotle in his *Metaphysics.* Concerning the position of
the liar, Aristotle asserts that with such a person you can discuss
nothing, for "he is saying nothing." Despite the missing references
to such classical sources, medieval thinkers were clearly the first to
expound fully the theory of *cassatio* through the careful consideration of statements such as "I do not speak" and "I am silent."

Another approach to the problem taken by the medieval scholastics involved a consideration of the self-referential nature of insoluble statements. Several medieval logicians, among them Albert of
Saxony and William of Ockham, maintained that no part of a proposition may be used to substitute for the whole proposition; that is,
the part can never be used to signify the whole of which it is a
part. As Ockham notes, a statement that contains the terms *true* or

false cannot be included in the range of reference of those terms. This view would seem to imply a type of hierarchy of languages, although no medieval commentator explicitly makes such a claim.

One of the most interesting analyses of the liar paradox during this period was made by Pierre d'Ailly, who wrote a special treatise on the *insolubilia* in the late fourteenth or early fifteenth century. D'Ailly began his analysis by distinguishing, as did Ockham, between three types of propositions: vocal, written, and mental. According to D'Ailly, a mental proposition is one that signifies, or expresses its meaning, in a natural manner, and no mental proposition can assert anything about itself, including its own truth or falsity. However, a mental proposition can be true or false depending on how it accords with the real world.

On the other hand, vocal and written propositions, according to D'Ailly's analysis, signify conventionally and are always subordinate to mental propositions. D'Ailly argues that the contradictions of the *insolubilia* are caused by the fact that we can use a vocal or a written proposition to attribute truth or falsity to a mental proposition and that we then confuse the two. Thus, as the French logician Anton Dumitriu has noted in his comparative study of scholastic and contemporary solutions to the semantic paradoxes, "The solution of Peter of Ailly shows, therefore, that the truth values of a mental proposition cannot be expressed in the same system of mental propositions but only in another system which speaks of these mental propositions, as does the system of written or oral propositions." This view is similar in some respects to contemporary solutions to the liar paradox and other logical paradoxes which involve notions of language levels or metalogic.

The first serious modern attempt to resolve the paradox of the liar was put forth by British philosopher Bertrand Russell. Russell argued that all paradoxes of the liar type, as well as his own set paradoxes and Kurt Grelling's paradox of heterologicality, are caused by vicious circularity. The vicious circles of these paradoxes are generated by the fact that we are asked to suppose that a set can contain members that can be defined only by means of the set itself. In his theory of types, Russell claimed that these paradoxes can be avoided if we are willing to reject statements that produce such vicious circles as meaningless; that is, as neither true nor false.

Russell (and later the German-American philosopher Rudolf Carnap) developed a more precise formulation of the theory of types (called the "ramified theory of types") by distinguishing between different *types* of propositions. For example, if x and y are objects, they are labeled $type_0$. If we talk about these objects—for instance, if we say "x is black" or "y is old"—then we are dealing with properties of the objects ($type_1$). It is also possible to talk about the properties of properties of objects ($type_2$) in such statements as "Black is a color property" and "Old is a temporal property." However, according to Russell's ramified theory of types, propositions such as "Black is old" would be considered meaningless and inadmissible, for the truth or falsity of a proposition of the type n can be discussed only in a proposition of the type $n + 1$.

Russell's theory seemed concerned only with averting the paradoxes by means of the principle of vicious circularity which rendered such statements meaningless. The theory did not identify the logical fallacy that was responsible for the vicious circularity encountered in the liar paradox. It was another suggestion made by Russell—that the concepts of truth and falsity also be arranged in a hierarchy—that proved a fruitful course of investigation by other logicians and mathematicians, most notably the Polish-American Alfred Tarski.

Tarski's analysis of the liar paradox is superior to Russell's in its formal methods. It involves, as Tarski puts it in a 1969 article "Truth and Proof," "a sharp distinction between the language which is the object of our discussion and for which in particular we intend to construct the definition of truth, and the language in which the definition is to be formulated and its implications are to be studied. The latter is referred to as the metalanguage and the former as the object-language."

Tarski begins with the notion of truth; he defines a sentence as true if it denotes the existing state of affairs and as false if it does not denote the existing state of affairs. This view, the semantic or classical conception of truth, is very close to that expressed by Aristotle in his *Metaphysics*. Tarski then asks us to consider a sentence similar to this one:

(1) The sentence printed on page 80, lines 37–38, of this book is false.

He abbreviates this sentence using the symbol "*s*." By checking that
(1) is, in fact, the sentence printed on page 80, lines 37–38, of this
book, it follows then that:

> (2) "*s*" is false if and only if the sentence printed on page 80,
> lines 37–38, of this book is false.

By our definition of truth, we can assert:

> (3) "*s*" is true if and only if *s*.

But "*s*" stands for the entire sentence (1). Therefore, we can substitute the entire sentence (1) into every occurrence of "*s*." By
doing this to the right side of (3), we obtain:

> (4) "*s*" is true if and only if the sentence printed on page 80,
> lines 37–38, of this book is false.

A comparison of (3) and (4) yields the contradiction:

> (5) "*s*" is false if and only if "*s*" is true.

Having presented the paradox in a formal manner, Tarski then
proceeded to demonstrate that it was impossible to construct a formal definition for truth or falsity "when the order of the metalanguage is equal to the order of the language itself." Tarski showed
that the concepts of truth and falsity cannot be rigorously defined
in the same order of language used to express them, but only in a
metalanguage. According to Tarski's analysis, the liar can speak
falsely in language L, but he can say nothing about the truth value of
the statement "I am lying" in language L. To talk about the truth
value of "I am lying," the liar must speak in language L_1. Without
specifying precise language levels, the liar's statement is being both
used and mentioned, and this ambiguity is sufficient to help generate
the paradox. Tarski asserts that all natural languages are essentially
inconsistent in this way, and the liar paradox is really just a re-
minder of this fact.

The relationship between Tarski's hierarchy of languages and the
Austrian-American mathematician Kurt Gödel's famous theorems
dealing with the incompleteness of arithmetic has been pointed out
by many commentators. In 1931 Gödel proved that it is impossible
to formulate a complete and consistent axiom system for arithmetic.
Such a statement on the surface appears to have nothing to do with

the liar paradox or with Tarski's work; yet, a quick survey of the background of the problem of consistency and the nature of formal proof makes the connections self-evident.

It was the ancient Greeks who first developed the axiomatic method, the most famous example of which is Euclidean geometry. All elementary geometry is said to be reducible to a few primitive terms called "axioms," which are accepted without proof. By properly using the rules of deductive reasoning, it is possible for one to derive from the axioms other true propositions of geometry called "theorems." If one assumes that the axioms are true, then the truth and the consistency of all the validly derived theorems can be guaranteed. Although the axiomatic method had a powerful impact on subsequent mathematical and scientific thought, only Euclidean geometry actually had what is considered to be a solid grounding in axiomatic theory.

It was not until the second half of the nineteenth century and the discovery and study of non-Euclidean geometries that mathematicians began to apply the axiomatic method to other areas of mathematics. The axiomatization of mathematics, as this process is called, spurred the formalization of mathematics, wherein formal signs and formulas are used to stand for the axioms and theorems of ordinary language. In a formalized theory, formulas are derived from others by means of the rules of logic accepted within the system. What is different between axiomatization and formalization is that the latter relies only on the shape or structure of the formulas and the rules applied to them; no ordinary language meaning is involved. As Tarski notes, "It is now known that all the existing mathematical disciplines can be presented as formalized theories. Formal proofs can be provided for the deepest and most complicated mathematical theorems, which were originally established by intuitive arguments."

By the turn of the century, the problem of consistency was a central concern of mathematicians, for if propositions such as Euclid's parallel theorem and its negation could each be taken as true (though not under the same system of geometry), then it appeared that theorems were no longer *necessarily* true. Furthermore, there is no certainty that if logical rules are correctly applied to meaningful variables, then no contradiction will be generated.

Many mathematicians, including the German David Hilbert and the American John von Neumann, were able to formulate consistency proofs for certain areas of mathematics, but these were basically *relative* consistency proofs: that is, proofs which showed, for example, that one system of geometry is consistent if another system of geometry is consistent. It was the German Gottlob Frege who demonstrated the importance of establishing an absolute consistency proof for arithmetic, and this need became more pressing as the consistency of other areas of mathematics was shown to be reducible to that of arithmetic. Frege, it may be recalled from "The Barber Paradox," was stymied in his attempt to find an absolute consistency proof for arithmetic by Russell's set paradox of 1901.

Gödel proved that such a proof was impossible. Using a special numbering system, he showed that for any deductive system S, if the system S is consistent, there exists a well-formed statement G within the system that is not provable by the rules of system S. In terms of arithmetic, this means that there are arithmetical sentences that are true but cannot be proved true—at least, not by the axioms and logical rules of proof used in arithmetic. (Gödel also demonstrated that within any well-formulated number system S, a well-formed sentence not-G is false but also not provable.) In ordinary language, Gödel proved that any deductive system of number theory such as arithmetic contains a sentence that asserts "I am not provable."

Such a sentence initially may appear paradoxical because its form is similar to that of the liar paradox, but in fact the statement is not at all contradictory. This can be shown, as the American philosopher John Van Heijenoort notes in an essay on Gödel's theorem, by considering the statement "I am not provable" and by defining the notion of provable merely by asserting that no false sentence is provable. Thus, if the statement "I am not provable" were provable, then it would be false and, therefore, not provable. But if that is so, then it is not provable *and* true, for the statement asserts that it is not provable—which, in fact, is the case. Similarly, if we consider the negation of the original sentence ("I am provable"), then such a statement, using a parallel analysis, is false but also unprovable. As Van Heijenoort comments, "We skirt the paradox but never fall into it. . . . The only point that may cause some surprise is that we have to introduce a distinction between 'true' and 'provable.'* If we refuse to do so, the paradox of the liar reappears."

Gödel's conclusions are not dependent on specific axioms and rules of inference, as one might at first suppose. The outcome of the reasoning is essentially unchanged regardless of the specific properties of the formalized theory one uses. Thus, Gödel's theorem applies not only to arithmetic but almost universally to any formal theory that includes the arithmetic of natural numbers.

All solutions to the liar paradox discussed so far have attempted to resolve the problem within the framework of traditional two-valued logic. Many-valued logics have been developed that provide for other interpretations. Three-valued logics often have "true," "false," and some third value. For instance, under one three-valued logic, statements of the liar type are considered neither "true" nor "false," but a third value, "paradoxical" or "meaningless." Under another three-valued system of logic, liar statements are undecidable; that is, they have a truth value (they are, in fact, true or false) but we cannot know which. All three-valued logic approaches ultimately fail because they are subject to a strengthened form of the liar paradox, one which asserts, "This sentence is false or paradoxical."

Another modern view, promulgated by the British philosopher P. F. Strawson, takes an entirely different approach to the problem of the liar and to the entwined question of truth. According to Strawson, "true" is not primarily a descriptive term, as the classical correspondence theory maintains, but is rather a performative utterance, one which does not make a statement but instead performs an action—in this case, the act of agreeing or accepting the statement itself.

According to Strawson, to say "It is true that snow is white" is not to make a statement about another statement but merely to say "Snow is white" and to accept this statement. Strawson argues that saying that a statement is true is like saying "Ditto." In the case of the liar paradox, Strawson rejects the metalinguistic approach and

* This distinction involves the fact that, as Gödel showed, the set of provable sentences within a system *S* does not coincide with the set of true sentences within the same system.

maintains that to utter a statement such as "This statement is false" is equivalent to saying "Ditto" when no one has spoken.

Other contemporary philosophers, most notably Saul Kripke of Princeton University, have argued that Tarski's metalinguistic approach is flawed. They believe that, as our intuition tells us, there is just one word *true* and not a series of phrases $true_0$, $true_1$, $true_2$, and so on. Kripke demonstrates that many of our ordinary statements about truth and falsity can become paradoxical given certain empirical facts. He asks us to consider statements such as "All of Nixon's statements about Watergate are false," uttered by former White House counsel John Dean, and "All of Dean's statements about Watergate are false," uttered by President Nixon. Kripke then goes on to show that under the metalinguistic approach it would be impossible for *both* men to assign an appropriate truth value level to each other's statement. Consider, for example, that Dean's statement ("All of Nixon's statements about Watergate are false") has to be at one level higher than all of Nixon's statements. Similarly, Nixon's statement ("All of Dean's statements about Watergate are false") must be at one level higher than all of Dean's statements!

Kripke partially succeeds in developing a hierarchy of language levels (without subscripts) that presents a single, univocal truth predicate and which accounts for the liar statement. According to Kripke, statements of the liar type are paradoxical, but he is careful to define "paradoxical" not as some non-classical truth value but as *no* truth value.

Kripke's approach also involves the concept of groundedness. Imagine that you are trying to explain the meaning of the word *true* to an alien being who understands English well enough to communicate but who just does not have a familiarity with the word *true*. You might approach the problem by suggesting that a statement is true when a person has the right to assert it and a statement is not true when a person has the right to deny it. Having established this, the alien can now assert (based on his understanding of the word *true* and based on his observations) that

Snow is white.

And he can also assert that

"Snow is white" is true

and also that

" 'Snow is white' is true" is true,

and so on.

Kripke says that a statement is grounded if eventually in this process it gets a truth value. This occurs when the first point at which the set of true (false) statements is the same as the set of true (false) statements at the preceding level. For most statements such as "Snow is white," groundedness occurs almost immediately. Few statements are ungrounded, and fewer still are paradoxical. As the British philosopher Susan Haack notes in her discussion of Kripke's work in *Philosophy of Logics:*

> All paradoxical sentences are ungrounded, but not all ungrounded sentences are paradoxical; a paradoxical sentence is one that cannot consistently be assigned a truth value at *any* fixed point. This supplies some explanation of why 'This sentence is true' seems to share some of the oddity of 'This sentence is false', and yet, unlike the Liar sentence, is consistent. A truth value *can* be given to 'This sentence is true', but only *arbitrarily;* a truth value *cannot* consistently be given to 'This sentence is false'.

Kripke's approach is open to some criticism inasmuch as it is forced into a kind of neo-Tarskian rejection of the strengthened liar paradox. What is clear is that many of the modern solutions to the liar paradox do bear striking resemblances to several of the medieval solutions. It may be, as Paul Vincent Spade, an American expert on medieval *insolubilia,* has suggested, that there can be no real final solution to the liar paradox but rather that we can only continue to work out elegant variations of the same basic approaches. Yet, even so, the significance of the work of Russell, Tarski, Gödel, and now Kripke on the foundations of mathematics and metamathematical logic bespeaks the value of their attempts.

See also THE CROCODILE'S DILEMMA and THE LAWYERS' PARADOX.

PERSPECTIVE PARADOXES

On both visible sides of the cube shown in Figure 50, there is one vertical line being intersected by two other lines. One intersecting line is drawn at an oblique angle to the vertical line, and the other line crosses at a right angle. Which line forms the oblique angle and which the right angle?

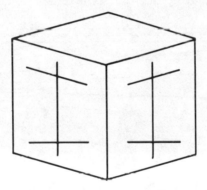

50. A perspective paradox.

It appears that the top line on each side is drawn at a right angle to the vertical line and that the bottom line is at an oblique angle. This analysis of the situation is based on what we *see;* in fact, the line situation is the opposite. The bottom lines are drawn at right angles and the top lines at oblique angles.

The perspective of the cube interferes with our perception of the angles of the lines on each surface. We assume the top line to be at a right angle to the vertical line because it appears to be parallel to the edge of the cube. This assumption is not poorly founded; after all, the edge of a cube must be at a right angle or we are not dealing with a cube. When we cover up the edges of the surface of the cube with paper, we are taking away the three-dimensional context of the cube—the context upon which we based our assumption. Now, what we have is a two-dimensional drawing of lines, and in this context the bottom lines are at right angles. Paradoxical perspective drawings often exhibit tension between two or more contrary perspectives.

Another well-known perspective paradox is produced by placing several figures of equal size on a perspective gradient (Figure 51). It then appears that the figure farthest away is about twice as large as the one nearest to us. Although we know that the figures are the same size, it is very difficult to perceive the situation as such because of the three-dimensional context created by the perspective lines. If these lines are removed, the equivalence of the figures becomes obvious.

51. Perspective gradient illusion.

The two perspective paradoxes presented so far rely on our intuitive understanding of the principles of central perspective. These principles were formally set down and their applications to drawing and painting first fully achieved by Italian Renaissance artists in the early fifteenth century. The technical aspects of the central per-

spective system can be easily grasped by considering a well-known
woodcut made by Albrecht Dürer in 1525 (Figure 52). The woodcut, called *Demonstration of Perspective*, is from the artist's treatise
on geometry and shows a device created by Dürer for making accurate central perspective drawings. In the woodcut, the straight
line of sight is indicated by a string, which is attached to the lute
and passes through an imaginary "picture plane" and is attached to
the wall by an eye hook. The hook represents the position of the
artist's eye when he drew the picture. The man to the right makes a
mark on the drawing board (hinged to the frame) that corresponds
to the point where the string crosses the picture plane. The man on
the left then moves the string to another position on the lute, and
the man on the right marks another corresponding point on the
drawing board. In this way, the outline of the lute can be represented in accurate central perspective.

52. Demonstration of Perspective, *by Albrecht Dürer.*

According to the central perspective system, horizontal and vertical lines that run parallel to the picture surface must be shown as horizontal and vertical lines. The artist also must represent equal distances along or between these lines as equal distances in the picture. Furthermore, objects appear to get smaller the farther away they are, and parallel lines appear to converge at distant vanishing points. It was the discovery and formulation of these and other principles by the Florentine architect Filippo Brunelleschi and other Italian artists that transformed Western painting.

As artists became more familiar with the techniques of central perspective, they were able to break its rules to create some startling perspective paradoxes. For example, one of the oldest types of perspective paradox is the anamorphosis, a drawing that presents a distorted image which when viewed at a sharp angle or when reflected on a proper mirror surface can be seen in its natural perspective. One of the earliest known examples of an anamorphosis was drawn by Leonardo da Vinci about 1485 (Figure 53).

53. Da Vinci's anamorphosis.

Da Vinci's image can be seen in correct perspective if viewed from the proper angle. To do this, put one thumb at the bottom of this page and close the book as far as you can. Then close one eye and view the image straight on with your open eye aligned more or less with the edge of the page. Not only will the image come into perspective but, as Da Vinci notes, it will appear almost to rise from the page. This characteristic of an anamorphosis was put to great effect by later artists.

The theory behind anamorphic art is a logical extension of the Renaissance discovery and exploration of the world of central perspective. With a representational picture drawn using central perspective, the viewer is able to coordinate his position in space relative to the picture's space. However, with an anamorphic picture, the artist paints from a single viewpoint which the observer must re-create in order to view the image in perspective.

Da Vinci offers the following guide for constructing a perspective anamorphosis:

Take an iron plate with a small round hole in the center. Put a light close behind it so that the light shines through the hole. Then place the object or figure you wish to draw directly against a wall. Draw an outline of the shadow on the wall or trace it on paper; then, fill in the proper details and shading. Have the person who is to view the drawing look through the same hole or at the same angle as the original light source. If you wish to make an anamorphosis of a perspective drawing, you need only make pinholes through the key lines and then pass light through at the desired angle and trace the resulting shadow.

Because a distorted anamorphic image is barely recognizable when viewed conventionally, it is not surprising that anamorphoses were often used to represent themes that involved or required some element of deception. Consider, for example, the two woodcuts by the sixteenth-century German artist Echard Schön, a student and follower of Albrecht Dürer (Figures 54 and 55). Figure 54 is entitled *What Do You See?* Viewed conventionally, one can

54. What Do You See? by Echard Schön.

see at the upper left portion of the picture Jonah being spat out of the whale that had swallowed him and just right of the center a whaling boat with three men in pursuit of another whale. When viewed at a sharp angle from the left edge of the paper, we can see the ribald scene of a man relieving himself and unsuspectingly about to be hit by a ram. In the woodcut called *Out, You Old Fool,* (Figure 55) the conventional view shows an old man making ad-

55. Out, You Old Fool, *by Echard Schön.*

vances to a young woman who, in turn, is stealing his money and handing it to her young lover, while a fool looks on from the other side of the bed. When viewed at an extreme angle, we see the inevitable outcome of such a situation as the old man is dispensed with and the young lovers go about their business.

Perhaps the most famous of all anamorphic paintings is *The Ambassadors*, painted in 1533 by the German artist Hans Holbein the Younger (Figure 56). The painting, which hangs in the National Gallery in London, is a double portrait of Jean de Dinteville, the French ambassador to the English court, and his fellow envoy and friend Bishop Georges de Selve. The precise, detailed renderings of the figures and the objects around them stand in stark contrast to the elongated, ambiguous image that appears on the floor between them. When this image is viewed from the left at eye level close to the wall of the museum on which the painting hangs, as in Figure 57, it is immediately clear that it depicts a human skull.

Some critics have suggested that Holbein is giving a hint of De Dinteville's impending death at the court. The painting is filled with symbols of the transience of human life, including the half-hidden crucifix at the upper left corner and the brooch of De Dinteville's hat which is decorated with a skull on a shield. Other art critics have indicated that the skull itself may be a visi-verbal pun on the painter's own name, as a skull could be described in German as a *hohl Bein*, meaning "hollow bone."

In the seventeenth century the first reflective cone and reflective cylinder anamorphoses were created. When the cone or cylinder of reflective material was placed in the center of the anamorphosis, the hidden image would appear in correct perspective on it. Interest in cone and cylinder anamorphoses grew in the late seventeenth and

56. The Ambassadors, *by Hans Holbein the Younger.*

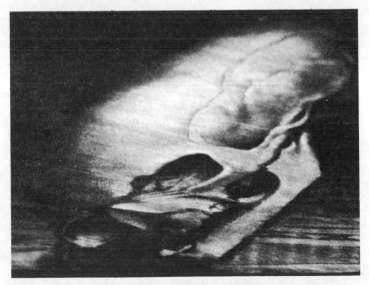

57. Detail from The Ambassadors.

58. A cylinder anamorphosis. Sleeping Venus Uncovered by Amor, *by Henry Kettle.*

eighteenth centuries, and numerous ones were made by artists in many European countries, including England, France, Germany, and the Netherlands. Figure 58 shows an eighteenth-century cylinder anamorphosis, *Sleeping Venus Uncovered by Amor*, by the English artist Henry Kettle.

Interest in anamorphic art reemerged in the late nineteenth century. An example from this period is the 1870 drawing of a castle by the Dutch artist J. W. Schwenck (Figure 59) in which the unique anamorphic characteristics of an object appearing to leave the page and seeming to be three-dimensional are fully achieved. You can experience this extraordinary illusion yourself by placing the tip of your nose just at the tab drawn at the bottom of the picture and looking up at the drawing while keeping the book on a horizontal plane.

The eighteenth-century engraving by the English master William Hogarth shown in Figure 60 was used as the frontispiece for his formal study of perspective. It points up the importance of following the rules of central perspective by poking fun at them through the impossible connections that are presented. For example, there is the placement of the rod and line of the fisherman in the right

59. Schwenck's castle anamorphosis.

foreground beyond that of the boy sitting on the bank and also beyond the woman at the window giving a light to the man on the hill. All these connections involve the illusion of depth within the picture plane. Hogarth succeeds in connecting people and objects

60. Hogarth's perspective paradox.

when the distance between them—if true central perspective had been followed—would be much greater than that represented. Nevertheless, the overall shape and first reading of the picture is coherent.

The Dutch artist M. C. Escher created several very complicated perspective paradoxes. For example, in his 1947 lithograph *High and Low* Escher uses the same vanishing point as both the zenith and the nadir (Figure 61). If we view the bottom half of the print first, we find ourselves looking up at a piazza. On a staircase to the left is a boy looking upward toward a girl at a window. All the vertical lines in the print curve upward, forcing our eyes to the center of the print where we see a tiled ceiling.

It is here that our perspective suddenly changes, for while the ceiling is the zenith of our view from the bottom of the drawing, it immediately becomes the floor and the nadir of the view presented in the top half of the drawing. Suddenly we find ourselves looking down at the piazza. There to the left is the boy sitting on the staircase looking up at the girl. Notice that in this portion of the lithograph, all curved lines move downward to the same tiled area, which this time serves as the ground. In fact, there are really three tiled areas in the print: the one at the bottom, the one at the top, and the one in the middle, which can serve as either zenith or nadir.

It is the ambiguity of this central tile area that creates the perspective paradox. We can see telltale signs of the contradictory forces that would come into play if such a structure existed. For example, notice that we can take the stairway down into the tower at the center right of the picture. However, if we do, we had better watch our step, because this must be a very strange place. We know this because the wall that connects with the tower entrance has a window that appears upside down. This window makes perfect visual sense when we see it from the bottom of the drawing, for then it is only one of several windows properly oriented. But, if we are to believe the drawing, it exists on the same level as the arched entrance and staircase to the tower. Therefore, somewhere there must be a boundary line between up and down. In reality, this boundary is the vanishing point which has been put to two different uses.

Escher created a somewhat more complex perspective paradox in his 1947 wood engraving *Other World* (Figure 62). In the center of the picture we see a creature that is half-man and half-bird, sitting on the sill of an arched opening. Behind the creature is a bleak alien landscape. This section of the engraving has a common horizontal perspective in which the vanishing point is on the horizon of the landscape. If you shift your eyes to the bottom of the engraving, you see the vanishing point as the zenith; you are looking up at the creature and the background is some unfamiliar part of the sky. The view from the top of the engraving uses the vanishing point as the nadir, and we look down at another creature.

61. High and Low, *by M. C. Escher.*

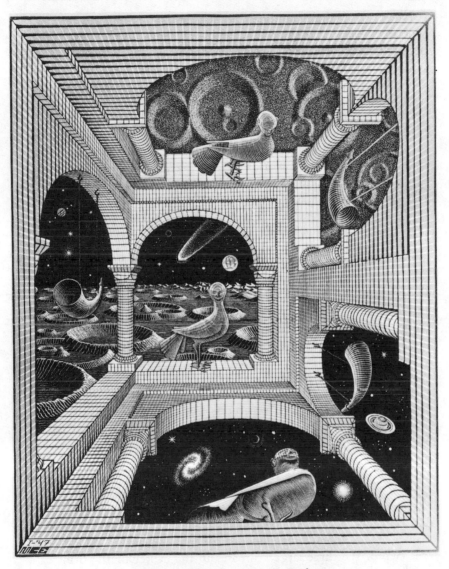

62. Other World, *by M. C. Escher.*

Notice that the wall lines in the horizon view are vertical, whereas they are horizontal in the other views. In the case of the horizontal wall lines, the lowest line for the zenith perspective is the highest for the nadir view. Likewise, the upper part of the arch structure from the zenith view is also the floor in the horizon view. The wall lines and the three pairs of corner windows reinforce each perspective and help to unify the drawing.

In a 1953 lithograph *Relativity* Escher uses three different vanishing points to create a unified picture that represents simultaneously three distinct worlds (Figure 63). If we look at the bottom center of the print, we see a featureless humanoid walking up a staircase. If the creature bears to the left, he will climb another staircase and find a garden in front of him and two staircases to either side of him. Each staircase is being used by other creatures oriented in the same world as he is.

If we return to our starting point at the bottom center of the drawing and look upward to the right, we notice something odd. Here is another humanoid, this one carrying a tray with a tumbler and a bottle, who appears to exist in a space that is oriented at a 90-degree angle to the first group of creatures. Several other creatures inhabit this second world, including one who is sitting beside a staircase reading a book, another who is climbing a staircase, and two who are having a meal at an outdoor table.

The third group of creatures also appear oriented at a 90-degree angle to the first group of creatures, but this time oriented to the left. One of these left-oriented humanoids is seen carrying a basket. Other left-oriented humanoids include one carrying a sack, one descending a staircase, an observer, and a couple walking off into a garden.

Each group of creatures inhabits a perfectly consistent world, one in which those humanoids oriented in another direction appear odd. Upright doors for one group become trap doors for others, walls become floors, ceilings become walls, and so on. Notice also that two of the three large staircases in the center of the print can be climbed on both sides. Because the vanishing points lie well outside the picture space, Escher is able to use these details to present a unified view of this curious world, a world in which three different planes can serve as the ground.

The situation presented by Escher has some parallels in the real

63. Relativity, by M. C. Escher.

world of space exploration. Without gravity, any plane in space can be the ground; hence, it would be possible for three astronauts to assume at the same time the three basic orientations shown in the print. However, in the space situation, there is no gravity involved, whereas Escher in his lithograph would have us believe that three different forces of gravity are at work at the same time.

Perhaps the most elaborate type of perspective paradox involves the construction of three-dimensional objects that produce ambiguous images. The American psychologist Adelbert Ames is best known for his perspective paradoxes involving a room and a chair,

64. The Ames room.

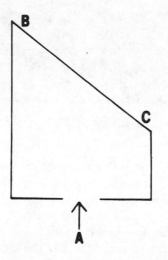

64a. Diagram of the Ames room. The perspective paradox is achieved only when viewed from point A. The difference in depth between A–B and A–C becomes evident when one's viewing point is shifted.

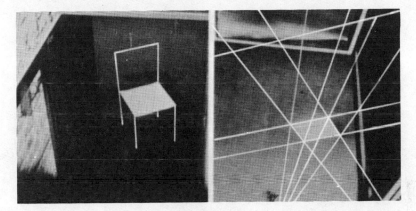

65. Two views of the Ames chair.

both of his design (Figures 64 and 65). When viewed from one point, the Ames room presents the image of an ordinary rectangular room. In fact, this room is quite distorted. The rear wall at the left corner is twice as distant from us as the rear wall at the right corner (Figure 64a). This difference in distance accounts for the illusion in which the young boy appears taller than the adult man, when actually the opposite is the case.

The Ames room appears normal from only one point. If we shift our angle of view, then the distortion of the room becomes evident and the paradox is eliminated. This is also true of the Ames chair (Figure 65), an object which when viewed from the correct point looks like a chair, but is in fact a collection of wires and a quadrilateral.

According to the British psychologist R. L. Gregory, Ames's research seems to indicate that every three-dimensional object presents an ambiguous retinal image, one which can be interpreted logically in two or more ways. What seems really paradoxical, according to Gregory, is how the brain can so readily identify the objects we see around us.

See also AMBIGUOUS FIGURES, M. C. ESCHER'S PARADOXES, IMPOSSIBLE FIGURES, and VISUAL ILLUSIONS.

THE PREDICTION PARADOX

Imagine a superior being—an omniscient god or a superintelligent computer—that can predict your choices in a particular game with *almost* total accuracy. The game involves two boxes that the Being places before you and a nice sum of money that will be yours if you win the game. You are given two options: either to take what is in both boxes or to take what is in Box 2. What is in the boxes depends on what the Being predicts you will do; the Being can make one of two predictions:

1. If the Being predicts that you will choose both Box 1 and Box 2, then it will put $1,000 in Box 1 and nothing in Box 2.
2. If the Being predicts that you will choose only Box 2, it will still put $1,000 in Box 1, but it will now put $1,000,000 in Box 2.

If the Being predicts your choice correctly, and as far as anyone knows he always has predicted correctly, you stand to win either $1,000 or $1,000,000. But it is theoretically possible, though unlikely, that the Being will predict your choice incorrectly. In that case, either of the two following outcomes will result:

3. If the Being predicts that you will choose both boxes and you choose only Box 2, then you end up with nothing.
4. If the Being predicts that you will choose only Box 2 and you choose both, then you get the $1,000 in Box 1 *and* the $1,000,000 in Box 2, for a total of $1,001,000.

The Being explains the game to you and the four possible outcomes, adding that its prediction has already been made and the money placed in accordance with this prediction. Now it is up to you to make the choice which will return you the largest amount of money. What is the most logical choice for you to make?

It may seem at first that there is no paradox here, just a simple question of choice. However, the paradox lies in the fact that a perfectly rational and equally strong argument can be made for either choice. According to Robert Nozick, a Harvard professor of philosophy, the problem thus becomes one of determining why one of these arguments *cannot* be legitimately applied to the choice in this situation.

It was Nozick who first brought the paradox, originated by William A. Newcomb, a physicist at the University of California's Livermore Laboratory, to the attention of philosophers, mathematicians, and scientists. Nozick, who presented the problem to a large number of people, including friends and students, asserts that people seem to divide evenly on the choice, with the proponents of each choice adamant about what makes perfect sense in this situation. The arguments go like this:

If you take both boxes, the Being, having almost certainly predicted this, will have put $1,000 in Box 1 and nothing in Box 2; thus, you would end up with $1,000. On the other hand, if you take only Box 2, the Being, having almost certainly predicted this, will have put $1,000 in Box 1 and $1,000,000 in Box 2; thus, you would almost certainly get $1,000,000. Quite obviously, it is preferable for you to take only Box 2, for almost certainly receiving $1,000,000 is better than almost certainly receiving $1,000.

However, one can also argue that the Being has already made his prediction; consequently, he has already put into Box 2 either the $1,000,000 or nothing. Thus, the content of Box 2 is already determined. This being the case, the following outcomes are possible: if the Being has already put the $1,000,000 in Box 2 and you choose both boxes, you get not only the $1,000,000 in Box 2 but also the additional $1,000 in Box 1. Moreover, if the Being put only the $1,000 in Box 1, you are still better off taking both boxes, for if you took only Box 2 in this situation, you would end up with nothing.

Let us furthermore rule out specious solutions to the problem —for example, the idea that you would make the choice by some random method rather than getting caught up in the logic of the Being's alternatives. Let us assume that if you choose randomly, the

BEING

		Predicts that you will take only what is in Box 2	Predicts that you will take what is in both Box 1 and Box 2
YOU	Take only what is in Box 2	$1,000,000	$0
	Take what is in both Box 1 and Box 2	$1,001,000	$1,000

66. Payoff matrix for Newcomb's paradox.

Being knowing this will leave $1,000 in Box 1 and nothing in Box 2, the same outcome as if you took both boxes. Consequently, it is definitely not to your benefit to choose randomly. Likewise, we can rule out the idea that there is any backward-in-time causality that would permit the Being to change its choice after hearing yours.

The basic contradictions involved in the paradox become evident if we construct a matrix of possible outcomes in the problem and then analyze the payoffs. Figure 66 presents such a payoff matrix.

Most analyses of Newcomb's paradox involve an application of game theory. Game theorists point out that the dilemma in choice here represents a conflict between two important principles of game theory: the expected utility principle and the dominance principle. The expected utility principle maintains that when faced with several available choices, a person should make the choice that brings him or her the maximum expected utility, which in this case is money. According to the principle of expected utility, taking only Box 2 is the most rational choice. Of course, the payoff matrix assumes that the Being is 100 percent correct, whereas the statement of the problem indicates that the Being's predictions are made "with *almost* total accuracy." Even if we assume conservatively that there is a one-in-ten chance that the Being will predict incorrectly, then the expected utility of the payoff involved is still $900,000. This is higher than the other payoffs if the same probabilities are applied. In fact, choosing only Box 2 continues to maximize expected utility even if the probability that the Being will predict correctly is only slightly better than fifty-fifty.

Contrariwise, the dominance principle leads us to conclude that choosing both Boxes 1 and 2 is the rational choice. According to the dominance principle, if we suppose the world is divided into states such that relative to it, you benefit by choosing action A rather than action B in at least one state, then even if the choices are equal in all other states, action A is still the best choice. If you examine the bottom row of the payoff matrix for Newcomb's paradox, you will see that the choice of taking both boxes is dominant because, for each state, this choice gives you more ($1,000 more, to be exact) than you would receive if you took only Box 2. This conflict between the expected-utility principle (which tells you to take only Box 2) and the dominance principle (which tells you to take both boxes) is the driving force behind the paradox. Regardless of the fact that plausible arguments can be constructed for choosing on the basis of either principle, the paradoxical situation still results as long as the predictive probability of the Being remains somewhat better than half.

Nozick recommends that you take both boxes, whereas Newcomb himself felt that you would be smarter to take only Box 2. Other commentators have joined the ranks in supporting one or the other of these recommendations. Most often, their arguments are merely elaborate restatements of those presented above, although several have tried to relate the paradox to that of the age-old dilemma of determinism versus free will. If you believe that the Being is Godlike in its omniscience, then you are likely to choose only Box 2, although your "choice" in this case is merely an illusion. On the other hand, if you believe that there is some possibility, however small, that the Being may err and that you have some free will in the situation, then your best bet would seem to be to take both boxes.

Recently, an American decision-theory specialist, John A. Ferejohn, has demonstrated that if Newcomb's paradox is observed from a decision-theoretic viewpoint rather than from a game-theoretic one, the apparent conflict between the principle of dominance and the principle of expected utility vanishes. In decision theory, it is assumed that a choice made by a participant in a situation such as the one described by Newcomb does not result in one

STATE OF NATURE

	Being made correct prediction	Being made incorrect prediction
Take only what is in Box 2	$1,000,000	$0
Take what is in both Box 1 and Box 2	$1,000	$1,001,000

(YOU labels the two rows on the left side)

67. Payoff matrix for decision-theoretic model of Newcomb's paradox.

certain and specific outcome but rather in a collection of several possible outcomes with differing probabilities of occurrence. From a decision-theoretic viewpoint, it is no longer a case of your viewing the Being as making a prediction based on your choice but rather whether the Being's prediction was correct or incorrect. This shift in viewpoint produces a slightly rearranged payoff matrix which shows an unexpected solution (Figure 67).

The most obvious difference between the two payoff matrices is that in the earlier game-theoretic matrix the two best outcomes involved the Being's predicting that you would take only Box 2. In the decision-theoretic matrix, the two best outcomes depend on which state of nature prevails; that is, on whether the Being's prediction was correct or incorrect. Because of this, neither of your two choices dominates the other. Consequently, it is the principle of expected utility that must be applied, and thus to take only Box 2 is clearly the sensible choice. As indicated earlier, this is true as long as the probability of the Being making a correct prediction stays slightly better than 50 percent.

See also THE PRISONER'S DILEMMA and THE PARADOX OF VOTING.

THE PRISONER'S DILEMMA

The district attorney of a small town is holding two gunmen as suspects in an armed robbery case, even though he knows that there is not enough evidence against either suspect to bring the case to trial and to win a conviction. Being an experienced hand at the ways of the criminal justice system and the criminal mentality, the district attorney brings each man into his office and presents him with the same facts and choices.

The district attorney admits that he needs a confession from one of them in order to get a conviction. Without a confession from one, he would have to lower the charges to illegal possession of firearms, which carries a maximum sentence of one year. According to the district attorney's offer, if one man confesses but his partner does not, then the stool pigeon goes free and the other gets ten years for armed robbery. If both men confess, each will get reduced sentences of five years. The district attorney keeps the suspects separated, and they have no opportunity to communicate with each other. What should each suspect do?

At first, the solution to the problem seems quite simple: neither suspect should confess so that they both end up with the minimum sentence possible—one year. But consider the problem from the perspective of each suspect. Then, we find that for each the better strategy is always to confess, regardless of what the other suspect does. For example, if Suspect A confesses and Suspect B doesn't, then A goes free, which is A's very best possible outcome. On the other hand, if B confesses too, then A is still better off having confessed, for under the terms of the problem he would get five years instead of ten. The identical reasoning applies to Suspect B's situation. Yet, if both suspects behave "rationally," their behavior constitutes a double confession, which produces a much harsher punishment for both suspects than if neither of them had confessed.

This paradox was first identified in 1951 by Merrill M. Flood, a researcher at the Rand Corporation. The prisoner's dilemma version presented here was formulated by Albert W. Tucker, a professor of mathematics at Princeton University. The problem has generated a great deal of research in communication and game theory, especially in the study of cooperation and conflict resolution.

Like the prediction paradox, this problem can be reduced to a simple matrix (Figure 68). The matrix shows two suspects, A and B, each of whom has two choices: to confess or not to confess. Each row and each column has a pair of numbers; the first number is the number of years in jail that Suspect A would serve for each possible choice and the second number is Suspect B's sentence given each choice.

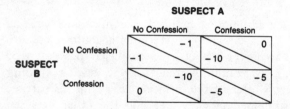

68. Payoff matrix for the prisoner's dilemma.

The top left box represents the payoff to each suspect if they follow the strategy of cooperation; that is, if neither of them confesses, each receives a sentence of one year. However, this choice is very unstable, for there is always the possibility that the other suspect will fall prey to temptation and double-cross his partner, thereby achieving the best possible individual payoff—freedom. In contrast, the lower right box shows the situation wherein both suspects confess and serve five years each. This situation, unlike the cooperative strategy, is in equilibrium; that is, there is no overriding reason for either suspect to prefer a strategy of no confession to one of confession. As indicated earlier, this is the situation regardless of what the other suspect does. Game theorists maintain that the dynamics of the situation lead each suspect to confess even though it will bring a harsher punishment than the strategy of co-operation and no confession.

Numerous gamelike experiments with real people playing the roles of the prisoners have shown that confession is the prevailing strategy adopted by participants. People who act on the cooperative no-confession strategy are consistently exploited by their partners. Those players who refuse to cooperate usually force the other player into a double-confession situation. Certain factors such as the relative length of the sentences and the number of games played have been shown to affect the outcomes. Cooperation is occasionally achieved in those situations where communication is permitted and there is an opportunity to develop trust between two players.

There are many examples of situations like the prisoner's dilemma in the real world. One frequently cited in international relations involves the arms race between two competing countries. Imagine that the two nations are already engaged in an arms race. Each country has the same choices: to continue to spend money on nuclear armaments or to stop. If both nations stop, then each can spend its money on projects that will benefit the people. If one nation continues to spend money on nuclear weapons and the other stops, then soon one will develop the military capability to defeat the other nation and thereby achieve domination. If both countries continue their arms buildup, they are both in effect worse off because they have spent enormous sums of money on dangerous nuclear weapons and neither is likely to be much stronger than the other.

But here, too, the most mutually beneficial strategy of cooperation is an unstable situation, one in which there is always the possibility of a double cross. Each country is thus pushed into a strategy of armament. The only way to break the pattern is through communication that provides an opportunity for the growth of trust between the nations. Within the context of the original conditions of the prisoner's dilemma, however, there is no solution to the problem unless one adopts a strategy that involves the use of meta-games.

The theory of metagames and its application to the prisoner's dilemma was first formulated in 1971 by an MIT social scientist Nigel Howard. A metasolution to the problem can be found if one extends the game to include one player's responses to the other player's possible strategies, the other player's responses to the first player's conditional strategies, and so on. In short, the game is extended in the sense that it now deals with metastrategies; that is, with selecting a rule to select a conditional strategy in response to the choice of strategy made by one's opponent.

For example, in the basic prisoner's dilemma game, each suspect has two choices: to confess or not to confess. Assuming Suspect B has these choices, then Suspect A has four metastrategies to consider: (1) he can choose not to confess regardless of what Suspect B chooses; (2) he can choose to confess regardless of what Suspect B chooses; (3) he can play tit-for-tat by choosing whatever strategy Suspect B chooses; or (4) he can play tat-for-tit by choosing the strategy opposite to that chosen by Suspect B. The choices involved in this situation are presented in Figure 69.

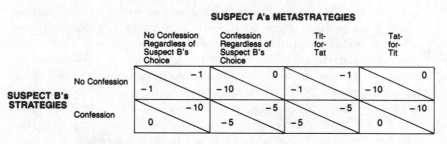

69. Payoff matrix for metagame version the prisoner's dilemma.

Thus, if Suspect B chooses not to confess regardless of Suspect A's choice and Suspect A always chooses not to confess, then the payoff is $(-1, -1)$. However, as in the original prisoner's dilemma game, this situation is unstable. The only time this situation is in equilibrium is if *both* confess. (In this case, both suspects receive the same payoff $[-5, -5]$, as in the original game.) The dilemma persists, both suspects play it safe, and both suffer a harsher punishment than if they had cooperated.

However, if Suspect B can predict Suspect A's metastrategies, then Suspect B can formulate his own metastrategies. For each of Suspect A's four possible metastrategies, Suspect B has four possible metastrategies, producing a total of sixty-four possible outcomes. In

SUSPECT A's METASTRATEGIES

	No Confession Regardless of Suspect B's Choice (N)	Confession Regardless of Suspect B's Choice (C)	Tit-for-Tat	Tat-for-Tit
1. N/N/N/N	(−1, −1)	(−10, 0)	(−1, −1)	(−10, 0)
2. N/N/N/C	(−1, −1)	(−10, 0)	(−1, −1)	(0, −10)
3. N/N/C/N	(−1, −1)	(−10, 0)	(−5, −5)	(−10, 0)
4. N/C/N/N	(−1, −1)	(−5, −5)	(−1, −1)	(−10, 0)
5. C/N/N/N	(0, −10)	(−10, 0)	(−1, −1)	(−10, 0)
6. N/N/C/C	(−1, −1)	(−10, 0)	(−5, −5)	(0, −10)
7. N/C/N/C	(−1, −1)	(−5, −5)	((−1, −1))	(0, −10)
8. C/N/N/C	(0, −10)	(−10, 0)	(−1, −1)	(0, −10)
9. N/C/C/N	(−1, −1)	(−5, −5)	(−5, −5)	(−10, 0)
10. C/N/C/N	(0, −10)	(−10, 0)	(−5, −5)	(−10, 0)
11. C/C/N/N	(0, −10)	(−5, −5)	(−1, −1)	(−10, 0)
12. N/C/C/C	(−1, −1)	(−5, −5)	(−5, −5)	(0, −10)
13. C/N/C/C	(0, −10)	(−10, 0)	(−5, −5)	(0, −10)
14. C/C/N/C	(0, −10)	(−5, −5)	((−1, −1))	(0, −10)
15. C/C/C/N	(0, −10)	(−5, −5)	(−5, −5)	(−10, 0)
16. C/C/C/C	(0, −10)	((−5, −5))	(−5, −5)	(0, −10)

Left axis label: SUSPECT B's METASTRATEGIES

70. *Metagame payoff matrix for Howard's version of the prisoner's dilemma.*

this expanded prisoner's dilemma game, there now emerge three equilibrium points (Figure 70). Two involve the payoff of (−1, −1), which is produced by both suspects' cooperation (no confession). In short, the cooperative behavior, which in the original prisoner's dilemma game was not stable, is in equilibrium in the metagame; that is, neither suspect can do better by single-handedly changing his strategy from one of no confession to one of confession. In ordinary language, these two new equilibrium points represent cooperative behavior. Suspect A's tit-for-tat strategy translates into ordinary language as "I'll cooperate if and only if you'll cooperate," and Suspect B's choice translates as "If that's so, then I'll cooperate with you."

Thus, each suspect's cooperation is conditional on the other suspect's cooperation. The reasoning behind this metasolution is logically unimpeachable; yet the solution also implies that there is some communication between the suspects. Indeed, once the suspects are able to communicate openly, they can develop cooperative strategies and the trust necessary to act on them. As noted by Anatol Rapoport, an American mathematician and expert in communication theory and the prisoner's dilemma:

> The key to the resolution of the paradox was the introduction of a new concept: that of conditional strategy. Howard's solution to the Prisoner's Dilemma is attractive because it was accomplished in the spirit of the method that has marked the steady maturation of logical and mathematical concepts. The method entails escaping from the conceptual framework in which a paradox or apparently unsolvable problem has appeared and putting the framework itself in a new perspective, so that the limitations of the old concept are revealed. Once the limitations are seen, a generalization of the concept suggests itself and a new framework can be constructed.

Steven Brams, an American political scientist and game theorist, has applied Howard's method to Newcomb's prediction paradox. Brams suggested that the Newcomb prediction paradox be reformulated so that we are dealing with two players, each of whom can predict the other's choices with almost total accuracy. Brams generalized the payoff matrix for each player and then combined them; the resulting payoff matrix is identical in its ranking of outcomes for both players to the payoff matrix for a two-person prisoner's dilemma game. In addition, the assumption that each player knows that his choices are almost certainly to be predicted accurately by the other player creates a situation in which a cooperative strategy is likely to prevail, if, as in the metagame solution to the prisoner's dilemma, a rule of conditional cooperation is adopted first by the leader and subsequently by the follower.

Unfortunately, despite Howard's metasolution to the prisoner's dilemma, it is difficult to see how the solution can be translated to real-world examples such as the nuclear arms race. It may be the ultimate tragedy of mankind that participants in arms limitation talks most often operate on the basis of strategies rather than metastrategies.

See also THE PREDICTION PARADOX and THE PARADOX OF VOTING.

PROBABILITY PARADOXES

British dramatist Tom Stoppard's 1966 play *Rosencrantz and Guildenstern Are Dead* opens with the two protagonists in a game of coin tossing. The hapless Guildenstern has tossed ninety coins in a row: all of them have come up heads and all have been duly surrendered to Rosencrantz. Despite the improbability of such a series of tosses, both Rosencrantz and Guildenstern are acutely aware of its real possibility. In fact, their game hints at one of the oldest and most important paradoxes of probability theory.

Let us remain with these two for a while, for they are both very fond of this sort of gambling game. When they grow tired of simply flipping coins, Rosencrantz suggests a variation: he will toss a coin until heads appears. If this occurs on the first toss, he will pay Guildenstern $1; if on the second toss, $2; if on the third, $4; and so forth, doubling the stake for each subsequent toss until the first heads appears.

The question is: what is a fair amount of money for Guildenstern to pay Rosencrantz for the opportunity to play this game?

The Swiss mathematician Nikolaus Bernoulli first posed this problem in 1713. It was modified and published later by Daniel Bernoulli, a nephew of its creator, in the *Transactions* of the St. Petersburg Academy, in Russia. If we apply the Bernoulli analysis to the situation described above, Guildenstern would have to pay Rosencrantz an infinite amount of money to make the game fair; in other words, there is no sum of money that would make the game fair. To understand why this is so requires consideration of the nature of games and the method for calculating probabilities of the type of events involved in the St. Petersburg paradox.

The basic problem of the theory of games is to determine how a player can obtain the maximum utility—that is, the most favorable result, which in this case is the largest sum of money. Other things being equal (which they never are), a person would behave rationally if and only if he acted in a way that would bring him the most gain; that is, Guildenstern wants to win as much money as he can from Rosencrantz, and vice versa. How do we calculate the odds for a fair game based on the payoffs described?

The probability that Guildenstern will get heads on the first toss is 1/2, because the coin must come up either heads or tails. Therefore, we can calculate the expected value for the toss at $0.50, since ½ × $1 equals $0.50. Now, suppose the first toss comes up tails and the second toss comes up heads. The probability that this sequence will happen is calculated by multiplying the probability of tails on the first toss (1/2) by the probability of heads on the second toss (1/2), which results in a probability of 1/4. The payoff involved in this situation is $2; thus the expected value to Guildenstern is also $0.50 (¼ × $2). The probability that the first heads will appear on the third toss is 1/8 (½ × ½ × ½) and the payoff is $4, once again resulting in an expected value of $0.50. It can easily be shown that the expected value for every toss is $0.50.

However, so far we have calculated only the expected value of each toss. To determine the expected value for the total game or series of games, we must add the values produced at each stage. We find that we are dealing with an endless series: ½ + ½ + ½ + . . . Regardless of the amount of money Guildenstern might pay Rosencrantz for the opportunity to play the game, Guildenstern still stands to win if he plays enough games. (Of course, this also assumes that both Rosencrantz and Guildenstern have an infinite amount of money to wager, and the time to keep on playing.)

Obviously, none of these assumptions can exist in the real world, which reduces the problem to an interesting though purely theoretical one—except for "doubling" schemes, which have a way of taking a finite number of victims every year.

If an infinite number of games cannot be played and an infinite amount of money cannot be wagered, what would constitute a fair wager against a finite bank of, say, $1 million? According to the British mathematician Eugene Northrop, it turns out to be the rather modest sum of $10.95.

Now, imagine that you have just walked into a casino in Las Vegas or Atlantic City and you observe a gambler playing a new card game. The game involves three cards: one is white on both sides, one is red on both sides, and one is white on one side and red on the other. Each card is concealed in a black slipcase. The banker permits the gambler to select one of the three black cases and to slip out the card and place it flat on the table so that only one side is visible. The side that shows is white, and the banker offers the gambler even money that the other side of the card is white. Should the gambler accept the bet? Why or why not?

The other side of the card must be white or red; hence, it seems logical that there is a fifty-fifty chance of the other side being white. Thus, the banker's bet of even money would appear to be fair. However, this is not the case, and if probability theory teaches us anything, it is not to accept our instincts when it comes to gambling odds.

We can see more readily why the odds are not fair if we specify all possible outcomes involved in the game. As we noted above, there are three separate cards, but the fact that we have picked a card with a white side does *not* mean that our two possible outcomes are equally likely, as our intuition would have us suppose. There are three white surfaces on the cards; one of them appears on the card with a red opposite surface and the other two are opposite faces of the same card: white$_1$-white$_2$, white$_2$-white$_1$, and white-red. Consequently, we can conclude that the probability that the other is white is two in three, which is considerably better than the odds the banker is giving the gamblers. The banker is sure to do well with this game in the long run.

The three-card paradox described above was formulated by Warren Weaver, an American mathematician, in 1950. It is a variation of a probability paradox originated by the French mathematician Joseph Bertrand in 1889. In Bertrand's box paradox, we are asked to imagine three identical boxes, each of which contains two coins. One box has two gold coins, one has two silver coins, and the other has one gold and one silver coin. It is obvious that the odds are 1/3 that the player will select the box with the two unmatched coins, for there are three equally probable choices and only one of them is favorable to the player. Yet, if we suppose that the player takes one coin out of the box selected and this coin is gold, then the probability seems to change; after all, there is only one coin left in the box and it must be either gold or silver, so the odds must be $1/2$.

To understand the error in our thinking we must go back to the gold coin we selected. Obviously, that first gold coin must have come from either the box with the two gold coins or from the box with the unmatched coins. The probability that we would select a gold coin as the first pick from the box with two gold coins is one in one, or certainty. The probability that the gold coin would be selected first from the box containing the unmatched coins is $1/2$. Now, if the first coin drawn is gold, then it is more likely that it came from the box with the two gold coins than from the box with the gold and silver coins. Similarly, if the first coin had been silver, then it would be less likely that it came from the mixed box than from the box with two silver coins. Thus, the probability that the second coin is unlike the first is less than the probability that it matches the first, regardless of what type of coin is drawn first. The probability is, as it was in the three-card paradox, one in three.

In certain situations specifying a detail in advance may change the probability of the outcome. Consider, for example, the paradox of the surprise ace, which is thought to have originated with the British mathematician Henry Whitehead of Balliol College, Oxford, in 1938. The original formulation involved a card game with a thirteen-card hand, but a four-card variation of the paradox makes the calculation of probabilities simpler while also making the crux of the paradox more obvious. (The variation presented here is that of Martin Gardner, the author of the monthly "Mathematical Games" column in *Scientific American*.)

Imagine a card game which involves two players and a deck of four cards: the ace of spades, the ace of hearts, the jack of diamonds, and the two of clubs. The cards are shuffled, and Player A draws two cards from the deck. Player A looks at his cards and announces, "I have an ace." What are the odds that he also has the other ace? As we can see in Figure 71 there are six possible hands in the game. Player A has already announced that he has an ace, so he must have one of the five hands that have aces. Thus, the odds are one in five.

Now, consider this situation. Suppose the two players agree in advance on a specific ace—for instance, the ace of spades—and

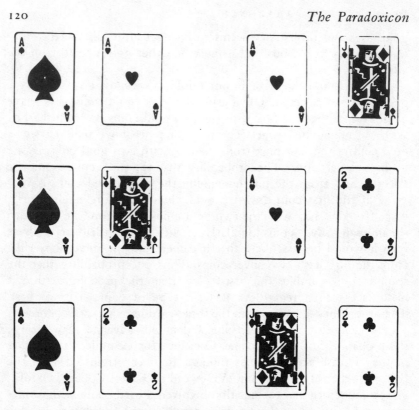

71. The paradox of the second ace.

then, after Player A has his cards, he announces that he does, in fact, have the ace of spades. What is the probability that he has the second ace? If you look again at the six possible hands, you can see that in this case Player A could only have one of three hands: ace of spades/ace of hearts, ace of spades/jack of diamonds, or ace of spades/two of clubs. Thus, the odds in this situation are one in three, which is somewhat better than in the first situation. Why should this difference in knowledge alter the probability in the two cases?

The difference in the two probabilities is dependent on the way the information is transmitted. In both cases, we are required to focus on a subset of all hands possible in the game, but the subset is larger in the first situation (five possible hands) than it is in the second (three possible hands). Of course, in both situations there is still only one hand in which Player A has both aces. It is important to note that two conditions must be met for the paradox to hold: both the named ace and the person who names the ace *must* be specified in advance, or there is no paradox.

A related paradox involves three prisoners who are in the same cell and who are condemned to die at noon on the next day. In the morning of the day of execution, a guard announces to the three prisoners that one of them has been pardoned. When asked which one it was, the guard replied, "I cannot tell a prisoner his own fate." Despite their repeated pleas, the guard remained silent. Prisoner A persisted and was able to talk to the guard with some privacy. He succeeded in convincing the guard that he would not be breaking the rules if he (the guard) told him (Prisoner A) which one of the two other prisoners—B or C—is certain to die. (At least one is certain to die.) The guard reasoned that it was acceptable because he would not be telling A his fate and he would not be telling the pardoned prisoner his fate. "Prisoner B is sure to die," said the guard. Prisoner A reasoned that since he was now certain that B would die then his chances for survival had improved from 1/3 to 1/2 and, indeed, they had!

The term *equiprobable* is an important one in probability theory; yet coming up with a precise definition of the term has been difficult. One group of mathematicians argues that two cases are equally likely if there is no reason to expect otherwise; that is, if we have no reason to prefer one outcome over the other, we are rational in believing that the odds of either occurring are equal. This is known as the "principle of insufficient reason," and it can lead to some rather startling conclusions. Consider, for example, the life-out-there paradox, also called the life-on-Mars paradox.

Imagine two scientists, one who believes in the principle of insufficient reason and the other who believes that we should consider two outcomes equally probable if and only if there is some reason to suspect that they are. (We might call this the "principle of sufficient reason.") Now, suppose that the believer in the principle of insufficient reason, call him Scientist A, is totally ignorant of any facts concerning the likelihood of life on other planets. His colleague, Scientist B, brings up the subject one day and asks A, on the basis of A's belief in the principle of insufficient reason, what the odds are that there are elephants on some other planet. Confessing total ignorance, Scientist A, the believer in insufficient reason, is forced to conclude that the probability is 1/2; that is, the events are to be considered equiprobable. Then his colleague asks what the probability is that there are cows on some other planet. Once again, the believer in the principle of insufficient reason is forced to conclude that the probability is 1/2. The challenger continues citing apes, camels, llamas, and so on, until he has listed twenty different life forms. This being the case, then the odds that all these things will *not* occur at once is about one in a million. (This figure is the product of multiplying the probability of each event: 1/2 $\times$ 1/2 . . . , up to twenty.) If the probability that *none* of these life forms exists on other planets is one in a million, then the probability that at least one of them does exist is nine hundred and ninety-nine thousand, nine hundred and ninety-nine in one million, or almost certainly!

The paradox here appears to be a *reductio ad absurdum* argument against the principle of insufficient reason. Indeed, assuming total ignorance of life on other planets and assuming that the occurrences of life forms are independent events—that is, that the occurrence of one is in no way related to the occurrence of another—the believer in insufficient reason is trapped in his own logic. However, these assumptions, although acceptable in a hypothetical world, are not possible in the real world, for we do know something about life out there and we also know that the occurrences of life forms are interrelated. Thus, having deflated the two key assumptions of the paradox, we are no longer justified in multiplying the probabilities of the individual events listed by the challenging scientist, and we can restore some of our faith in the principle of insufficient reason.

Another type of probability paradox involves the frequency of coincident events. Consider, for example, the birthday paradox. Imagine a room with two dozen people who do not know each other. The probability that any two persons' birthdays are different is 364 out of 365, for there is only one day on which their birthdays can match. Now, suppose someone is willing to bet you two to one that there are two people in the room with the same birthday. Should you accept the bet?

If you are like most people, it seems perfectly clear that you should not pass up your friend's bet, but this is not the case. In fact, the odds that in a room of twenty-four people there will be two people with the same birth dates is better than 50 percent. "How can this be?" you ask. "After all, look at the overwhelming odds in favor of two people having different birthdays."

To understand why the probability is better than two to one that there are two such persons in the room, it is necessary to know how the probability of events such as these are calculated. It is true that the probability that any two people will not have the same birthday is 364/365. (For the sake of simplicity we exclude any possible February 29.) However, the probability that a third person will not have a birthday identical to one of the other two is 363/365, since there are two possible days for it to match. Likewise, the probability that a fourth person would have a matching birthday is 362/365; a fifth, 361/365; and so on—until we have accounted for twenty-four possible birthdays, the last with a probability of 342/365. This series of fractions is multiplied, and it produces a probability of 46/100. This figure is the probability that among a group of twenty-four people there will be *no* matches; the probability that they will produce a match is obviously 54/100, or better than half.*

There are numerous ways that you can verify the startling outcome of the birthday paradox. In addition to getting twenty-four people together, you could check a reference work such as Who's Who or an almanac for the birth dates of twenty-four randomly selected individuals or groups of presidents, writers, inventors, and so on. There is a better than even chance that there will be one pair of matching dates. If you take a group larger than twenty-four, the probability increases as the size of the group increases. With a group of about thirty people, the odds are about 65/100 and with forty people, 90/100. In a group of a hundred people the odds that there are matching birth dates soars to more than three million to one!

The Russian-American physicist George Gamow, who discusses this paradox in his 1947 book *One, Two, Three . . . Infinity*, claims that he has presented the problem to a great many people, including

* The probability of at least two matching birthdays can be calculated for any number of people using this formula, where n equals the number of people:

$$1 - \frac{365 \times 364 \times 363 \times 362 \times \ldots \times (365 - n + 1)}{365^n}$$

a number of well-known scientists, and invariably they have thought that it was reasonable to accept the friend's bet. As Gamow notes, "The problem of coincident birthdays represents a very fine example of how a common-sense judgment concerning the probabilities of complex events can be entirely wrong."

A more startling counterintuitive problem is the small world paradox. Imagine that you are given a document and told that it is your task to get this document to a target person, who lives in a distant state but who is not personally known to you. Furthermore, in getting the document to your target person, you must follow these procedures: you must mail the document to someone whom you know personally and who you think is most likely to know the target person. The friend to whom you send the document must do likewise, sending it on to someone he knows personally, and so on. On the average, how many intermediate links do you think would be necessary to accomplish the goal?

The hypothetical experiment posed above actually has been performed a number of times under the direction of Professor Stanley Milgram, an American social scientist. Milgram found that most people estimated the number of necessary links to be about one hundred. However, the results of the experiment proved otherwise. In fact, the number of links between the starting person and the target person turns out to vary from two to ten links, with a median of five.

Another coincident probability paradox, somewhat less startling though equally as entertaining as the others, involves the birth date of the young hero, Frederic, in Gilbert and Sullivan's *The Pirates of Penzance*. Frederic, having been born on the twenty-ninth of February, is faced with the conundrum of how to determine his age. In delighted surprise, he sings:

> *How quaint the ways of Paradox!*
> *At common sense she gaily mocks!*
> *Though counting in the usual way,*
> *Years twenty-one I've been alive,*
> *Yet, reckoning by my natal day,*
> *I am a little boy of five!*

Quite obviously, Frederic is not five; yet, how do we reconcile his age if his birthday comes only once every four years? Frederic's paradox is what the American philosopher Willard V. Quine calls a "verdicular," or truth-telling, paradox—"one which has managed to sustain *prima facie* absurdities by conclusive argument." The force behind Frederic's paradox is merely the unexpected fact that it *is* possible for a person to be older than the number of birthdays he has had. Frederic, it turns out, is $4n$ years old on his nth birthday. This appears startling at first because it is such a rare occurrence in the real world—it has a probability of $1/1,460$!

See also STATISTICAL REVERSAL PARADOXES and THE PARADOX OF VOTING.

THE RAVEN PARADOX

While taking a group of benefactors on a tour through the new aviary they had just helped to build, a noted ornithologist commented, "And here we have two of the finest examples of ravens that I have ever seen. Notice the lustrous black plumage for which all ravens are famous." The ornithologist continued his lecture, commenting on the corvine feeding and nesting habits as well as on the birds' legendary role as harbingers of ill fortune.

When the ornithologist had finished, a young man said, "Sir, excuse me, but did you say that 'All ravens are black'?"

"I don't know if I said exactly that, but it's true. All ravens are black."

"But, how do you know that—for certain, I mean?" asked the young man.

"Well, I've seen a few hundred ravens in my day and every one of them has been black."

"Yes, but a few hundred are not *all*. How many ravens are there, anyway?"

"I would guess several million. As for your question, many other scientists, and non-scientists for that matter, have observed ravens over thousands of years and so far the birds have all been black. At least, I don't know of a single instance in which someone has produced a non-black raven."

"That's true, but it's still not *all*—just *most*."

"True, but there is other evidence. For example, take all these lovely multicolored birds we have seen today—the parrots, the toucans, the peacocks—"

"They're lovely, but what do they have to do with your claim that all ravens are black?"

"Don't you see?" asked the ornithologist.

"No, I don't see. Please explain."

"Well, you accept the idea that every new instance of another black raven that is observed adds to the support of the generalization that all ravens are black?"

"Yes, of course."

"Well then, the statement 'All ravens are black' is logically equivalent to the statement 'All non-black things are non-ravens.' This being so and because whatever confirms a statement also confirms any logically equivalent statement, it's clear that any non-black non-raven supports the generalization 'All ravens are black.' Hence, all these colorful, non-black non-ravens also support the generalization."

"That's ridiculous," chided the young man. "In that case you might as well say that your blue jacket and gray pants also confirm the statement 'All ravens are black.' After all, they're also non-black non-ravens."

"That's correct," said the ornithologist. "Now you're beginning to think like a true scientist."

Who is reasoning correctly, the ornithologist or the young man?

The raven paradox has been the subject of considerable debate among philosophers of science since the mid-1940s, when it was first brought to their attention by the German logician Carl Hempel in his paper "Studies in the Logic of Confirmation." The raven paradox, also known as the "paradox of confirmation," is a paradox of inductive logic and, consequently, does not involve a logical contradiction that has been validly drawn from a set of true premises. The raven paradox is paradoxical because the logical consequences of two principles of inductive logic—the principle of confirmation and the principle of equivalence—seem to produce logical consequences that are counterintuitive.

The imaginary dialogue between the ornithologist and the young benefactor has already provided an informal introduction to the principle of confirmation. All inductive logic seems based in part on the notion of confirmation; that is, that every generalization, such as "All ravens are black," is confirmed by *instances*. This means that every case of an observed black raven adds to the support of the generalization; the principle of confirmation states that the more instances, the better the support or the higher the degree of confirmation. In inductive logic, there is no such thing as certainty; one can only say that there is a great degree of evidential support for a generalization. On the other hand, a single instance of a non-black raven would be sufficient to disconfirm the *universal* generalization and reduce us to saying "most" or "some" ravens.

It is this shift from "all" to "most" or "some" that is of great significance to philosophers and scientists. Universal generalizations of the "All *P*s are *Q*s" type are the stuff upon which important scientific and mathematical systems are built. Either *all* planets revolve around the sun or we no longer have an important law of celestial motion, and a considerable portion of physics is lost as well.

More than the principle of confirmation is questioned by the raven paradox. As noted by the ornithologist, the principle of equivalence is also involved. Two statements are said to be logically equivalent if and only if when one is true the other is true and when one is false the other is false. In other words, logically equivalent statements always have the same truth value. Some philosophers say that this is because two logically equivalent statements—for example, "Either we won't get into the movie or it won't be good" and "It is not the case that we will get into the movie and it will be good"—are really saying the same thing. Other philosophers reject this notion entirely and maintain that logically equivalent statements merely have the same truth value. Regardless of one's view on the matter, the relevance of logical equivalence to the raven paradox is obvious. If two logically equivalent statements have the same truth value, it seems sensible that any instance that confirms one statement also confirms the other. Similarly, any disconfirming instance, such as a white raven or a blue one, would force us to reject both generalizations.

Although the principle of confirmation and the principle of equivalence are both perfectly plausible, it is the conjunction of the two in the case of the raven paradox that seems to produce the paradoxical effects that we experience. Of course, the problem for philosophers and scientists is to explain the paradox without rejecting either of these valuable principles—or at least, doing a minimum of damage to them. For a few, this has been too much to ask, and one or the other of these principles has been abandoned.

For example, The American logician Nelson Goodman in his 1955 book *Fact, Fiction, and Forecast* argues that certain restrictions be placed on the principle of equivalence. He suggests that we make it a necessary condition of confirmation that any observation or example offered as a confirming instance of the generalization of the "All *P*s are *Q*s" type cannot also confirm the statement that "No *P*s are *Q*s." This permits us to accept an instance of a black raven as a confirming instance of the statement "All ravens are black" but not a white handkerchief and a black pen, for inasmuch as these two examples are not instances of black ravens, they do add support to the statement "No ravens are black."*

In contrast to Goodman's approach to the paradox, most philosophers have "solved" the problem by maintaining that its source is not in faulty reasoning but in our mistaken intuition, which tells us that there is something illogical here. Philosophers who argue for this view usually claim that the closer we examine the problem, the less paradoxical it becomes. They would have us believe that the generalization "All ravens are black" can indeed be confirmed by instances of white doves, gray pinstripe suits, and rainbows.

Hempel and his supporters argue that the paradoxical effects of the raven paradox are produced in part by our misinterpretation of the scope of such universal generalizations. In ordinary language, we focus on the grammatical subjects (ravens, blackness, etc.) of these generalizations and, hence, we take them to be limited in scope. In fact, from a strictly logical viewpoint, they are unlimited in scope; that is, they are about *everything*. This becomes apparent when we realize that all these universal generalizations do is deny that certain characteristics or properties can be conjoined; for in-

* The British philosopher A. J. Ayer develops this point further in his 1972 book *Probability and Evidence*: ". . . The white handkerchief would still confirm the generalisation that all non-black things are non-ravens, but the black raven and the black fountain-pen would not, since they would also satisfy the generalisation that no non-black things are non-ravens. All three would confirm the third of our equivalent generalisations—that everything is either black or not a raven, since they all violate the hypothesis that nothing is either black or not a raven, but that is not paradoxical. What is suggested here is that we take advantage of the logical fact that whereas the propositions 'All ravens are black', 'All non-black things are non-ravens' and 'Everything is either black or not a raven' are logically equivalent, their respective contraries, in the Aristotelian square of opposition, 'No ravens are black', 'No non-black things are non-ravens' and 'Nothing is either black or not a raven' are very far from being so."

stance, the generalization "All ravens are black" denies that anything is a raven and non-black. It does not seem paradoxical that
every object we could identify—whether those listed above or yellow shirts, brown shoes, and so on, almost endlessly—will be either
a confirming or a disconfirming instance of the generalization.

Hempel argues that our reluctance to agree that there are things
that are non-ravens which support the generalization "All ravens
are black" seems largely based on the fact that we interpret these
generalizations with the benefit of previous knowledge. According
to Hempel, while we might find it odd to hold a piece of ice to a
flame in order to support the statement "All sodium salt burns yellow," we find it odd only because we know that ice is not sodium
salt nor does it probably contain sodium salt. We would not find
the procedure strange if we did not know exactly what it was we
were holding up to the flame. The fact that it did not burn yellow
and proved not to be sodium salt would then appear to be very
relevant to the confirmation of the generalization. It is our intuition
that tells us the existence of white doves, gray pinstripe suits, and
rainbows should not have any relevance whatsoever to our generalization about the color of ravens, and it is unassailable logic that
proves our intuition wrong, in Hempel's view.

Some philosophers, uncomfortable with such counterintuitive arguments, have sought to resolve the paradox by arguing that instances of non-black non-ravens provide a different level of support
for the generalization. Invariably, such arguments begin with the
idea that the set of ravens is considerably smaller than the set of
non-ravens or the set of non-black things. Theoretically, there are
three ways one could go about gaining maximum support for the
generalization "All ravens are black." One could examine all ravens
and determine that they are all black, one could examine everything
and determine there are no non-black ravens, or one could examine
all non-black things and determine that none of them are ravens. It
makes most sense to observe the ravens, which are considerably
fewer in number than non-black things or everything. It seems
plausible to say that the observation of a black raven provides more
support for the generalization than does the observation of a non-
black non-raven. This is so because a single observation of a black
raven represents a greater proportion of the set of all ravens than
does a single instance of a white dove to the set of non-black non-

ravens. As A. J. Ayer notes, "If the world were such that it contained a great many ravens and very few things that were not black, the sensible and more productive course would be to pick out the non-black things and see if any of them were ravens."

See also THE GRUE-BLEEN PARADOX.

THE SHOPKEEPER'S PARADOX

Peter is the owner of a shop. He works with two employees, Quentin and Ralph. Peter wants to make certain that the shop is never left unattended and, consequently, has ruled that the three men cannot be out at the same time. Peter, who is still weak from a recent illness, has also made it a rule that if he leaves the shop, then Quentin must accompany him.

Now, if you assume that if Ralph goes out, then, according to Peter's first rule, if Peter decides to go out, Quentin must stay in or the shop would be unattended. However, Peter's second rule states that if he goes out, then Quentin must go out as well. Thus, the initial assumption that Ralph goes out appears to lead to a false conclusion. Therefore, the assumption itself must be false; consequently, Ralph cannot ever leave the shop. Yet, this is an absurd conclusion, for it is obvious that when Peter and Quentin are in the shop or even when Peter is alone in the shop, Ralph can be out without violating any of Peter's rules. Is it logically possible for Ralph to leave the shop without violating any of Peter's rules?

An elaborate variation of this paradox was first presented by Lewis Carroll in the July 1894 issue of the British journal *Mind*. In the original paradox, two disputants, Uncle Joe and Uncle Jim, are on the way to a barbershop while arguing, respectively, that Ralph (it was Carr in the original) cannot leave the shop and that he is free to leave based on Peter's rules. The answer to the problem, which Carroll intended for the second volume of his *Symbolic Logic*, was a source of disagreement between the two original disputants, Carroll and John Cook Wilson, a professor of logic at Oxford. The dispute and the solution to the problem really turns on an understanding of material implication, a logical operation which is often used to represent ordinary language statements of the "if . . . then" type.

In formal logic, statements such as "If Peter is out, then Quentin is out" or "If Ralph is out, then if Peter is out, Quentin is in" are called conditionals and are usually symbolized as $p \supset q$. The p refers to the "if" part of the statement called the "antecedent," and the q symbolizes the consequent, or "then" part. In ordinary language, conditional statements such as "If it rains, I will stay at home" or those used in Carroll's paradox imply a causal connection of some kind. However, the horseshoe symbol $\supset$ used to represent material implication in formal logic does not imply *any* causality. Material implication simply asserts that any proposition of the form "$p \supset q$" is true if the antecedent is false (regardless of the truth value of the consequent) or if the consequent is true (regardless of the truth value of the antecedent). Thus, if we take the conditional statement "If Peter is out, then Quentin is out," and if the antecedent is true (Peter is out) and if the consequent is false (Quentin is in), then the conditional statement is false. However, this is the only case in which the conditional statement is false according to what is called "material implication." If the antecedent is false and the consequent is false or if the antecedent is false and the consequent is true, the truth value of the conditional is still true.*

This interpretation of "if . . . then" conditionals prevailed during Carroll's time and almost all systems of logic that developed at that time (and many in our own time) involve this meaning of material implication. This view of conditionals gives rise to what are called the "paradoxes of material implication." For example, the conditionals "If Ronald Reagan won an Academy Award for Best Actor (false), then the moon would be made of green cheese (false)" or "If Einstein said '$E=mc^8$' (false), then Ronald Reagan is the forti-

---

* This can be demonstrated by what logicians call a "truth table," a formal chart that shows all possible truth values for each propositional variable (p, q, etc.) and for the compound statements they form. As can be seen, the only time the compound statement "$p \supset q$" is false is when the antecedent is true and the consequent is false.

p	q	$p \supset q$
T	T	T
F	T	T
T	F	F
F	F	T

eth President of the United States (true)" are both considered *true* compound statements. The logic is simple: any statement of the form $p \supset q$ is false if and only if the statement substituted for p is true and the statement substituted for q is false.

As the British philosopher Bertrand Russell and other commentators on the problem have noted (and as Carroll argued), if we accept this meaning of material implication, then Ralph can indeed leave the shop without violating any of Peter's rules. Russell, who thought highly of Carroll's paradox, nevertheless commented on it quite succinctly in a footnote to *The Principles of Mathematics*. To paraphrase Russell, the only inference warranted by Lewis Carroll's premises is that if "Ralph is out" is true, "Peter is out" must be false, i.e., that Ralph is out implies "Peter is in," and this is the conclusion to which common sense leads us.

This view of material implication presents other counterintuitive notions. For example, it is possible to derive the theorem that "p implies q or q implies p," using the material conditional. The American logician C. I. Lewis has noted that this theorem can be construed as saying that if you take any two statements at random from a newspaper, you can validly argue that the first implies the second or that the second implies the first.

There is one final paradoxical footnote to the dispute between Carroll and Cook Wilson. Between late 1892 and 1894 Carroll wrote several other versions of the problem. Each successive reworking incorporated arguments and counterarguments posed by the two logicians. However, neither man publicly acknowledged whose views were represented by which characters. Uncle Joe in the paradox maintained that Ralph could not leave the shop, whereas Uncle Jim maintained that he could. From 1905, the year in which Cook Wilson published an article about the paradox in *Mind*, all commentators have assumed that Uncle Joe represented Carroll's views and that Uncle Jim expressed Cook Wilson's views. Recent Carrollian scholarship by the American logician William Warren Bartley III indicates that the opposite was the case. Bartley comments:

> During the controversy itself, both parties appear to have stuck to their positions; in the months that followed, however, *both* appear to have had second thoughts—although there is some doubt

that either would have conveyed these to the other. Cook Wilson gradually learned material implication, and even came to accept it, as shown by his *Mind* article of 1905. Carroll, on the other hand, began to wonder about the adequacy of material implication to express [conditional] statements.

See also THE CROCODILE'S DILEMMA and THE LAWYERS' PARADOX.

STATISTICAL REVERSAL
PARADOXES

Imagine that on the desk of a certain high-ranking Washington official are two jelly bean jars, one black and the other white. Each jar contains a mix of licorice and papaya-flavored jelly beans, the only two kinds this executive eats. At the moment under consideration, there are 50 licorice and 60 papaya jelly beans in the white jar. The black jar contains 30 licorice and 40 papaya jelly beans. If the executive wanted a licorice jelly bean and could only choose one without seeing it, from which jar should he choose in order to maximize his chances?

Now, imagine the same desk and the same jars, only this time the jars contain a slightly different assortment of jelly beans. The white jar contains 60 licorice and 30 papaya jelly beans. The black jar contains 90 licorice and 50 papaya jelly beans. Which jar should our executive choose from if he wanted to maximize the probability of selecting a licorice jelly bean?

In the first case, the probability of choosing a licorice jelly bean from the white jar is 50 to 110, which reduces to a 45 percent chance. The probability of drawing a licorice jelly bean from the black jar is 30 to 70, or a 43 percent chance. Consequently, the white jar offers the executive his best chance of getting a licorice jelly bean.

In the second case, choosing from the white jar once again gives the executive a better probability (60 to 90 or a 67 percent chance) than choosing from the black jar (90 to 140, or a 64 percent chance). None of this is particularly paradoxical; it just requires a simple mathematical calculation. But then, consider a situation in which the contents of the two white jars described above were mixed together and the contents of the two black jars mixed together. Which jar should the executive choose from in this situation if he wants to maximize his chances of selecting a licorice jelly bean?

Common sense tells you that if the white jar was the better choice for selecting a licorice jelly bean when dealing with the jars in the first two cases, then it should provide the better bet when choosing from the jars with the combined jelly beans in the third case. In other words, mixing the jelly beans should not change which jar provides the executive with the better chance of selecting a licorice jelly bean. Despite what common sense leads us to believe, however, this is not the case. It is the black jar which now provides the better chance of his choosing a licorice jelly bean. The white jar offers odds of 11 to 20, or a 55 percent chance, whereas the black jar offers odds of 12 to 21, or a 57 percent chance.

As this simple example demonstrates, it is possible for the data from two different cases considered separately to support the same hypothesis ("The white jelly bean jar offers the better odds for selecting a licorice jelly bean"), but when the data from the two cases are considered together, for them to disconfirm the hypothesis. This statistical fact of life may not be particularly troublesome when dealing with jelly beans, but it does have serious implications for medical, economic, and other types of research projects. Consider, for example, the following hypothetical medical study based on an example presented by Colin R. Blyth, a professor of mathematics at the University of Illinois. This type of problem is called Simpson's paradox, having been named after the British statistician E. H. Simpson, who first wrote about it in 1951.

A doctor wants to compare the effectiveness of a new treatment for a disease to that of the standard treatment. He is to make his tests in two locations, Alphaville and Betaville. A statistician advised the doctor to give the new treatment to 91 out of every 100 patients with the disease in Alphaville, to give the standard treatment to the other 9, but to make sure that the assignments were made on a random basis. He also advised the doctor to prescribe the new treatment to 1 out of every 101 Betaville patients and the standard treatment to 100 out of every 101, also on a random basis. The probabilities suggested by the statistician for assignment were expected to provide the doctor with approximately the number of patients he would need and could handle in each city.

After a year of collecting data the doctor summarized his results,

Effectiveness of Treatment	Alphaville patients		Betaville patients	
	Standard Treatment	New Treatment	Standard Treatment	New Treatment
Not Effective	950 (95%)	9,000 (90%)	5,000 (50%)	5 (5%)
Effective	50 (5%)	1,000 (10%)	5,000 (50%)	95 (95%)

72. *Simpson's paradox. The doctor's summary of the effectiveness of the new and standard treatments.*

as shown in Figure 72. He concluded on the basis of his statistics that the new treatment was very effective; in fact, almost twice as effective as the standard treatment.

The doctor sent a copy of his results to the statistician, who called the doctor immediately and criticized him for continuing with the new treatment when it was obviously such a bad one. The bewildered doctor asked the statistician on what basis he reached his conclusion and was presented with the summary shown in Figure 73.

Effectiveness of Treatment	Standard Treatment	New Treatment
Not Effective	5,950 (54%)	9,005 (89%)
Effective	5,050 (46%)	1,095 (11%)

73. *Simpson's paradox. The statistician's summary of the effectiveness of the new and standard treatments.*

According to Blyth, the doctor is on sounder footing than the statistician. Using the data that the doctor collected, one could expect to have had about 10,700 recoveries if all the patients had been given the new treatment instead of the actual 6,145. Had all the patients been given the standard treatment, one could expect the recovery rate to be 5,600. As Blyth notes in a 1972 article on Simpson's paradox:

> The difficulty is not one of chance variation—the observed proportions might be true ones, or the observed numbers could be multiplied by a constant large enough to make this essentially so. As with any paradox, there is nothing paradoxical once we see what has happened: The [Alphaville] patients are much less likely to recover, and the new treatment was given mostly to [Alphaville] patients; and of course a treatment will show a poor recovery rate if tried out mostly on the most seriously ill patients.

Consider another example of Simpson's paradox, this one relating to the effectiveness of a new medication on men and women. Two doctors in the study both report that the new drug is more effective on men than on women; their statistics are presented in Figure 74.

Effectiveness of Medication	Doctor A's Results		Doctor B's Results	
	Men	Women	Men	Women
Effective	2,000 (40%)	1,000 (33%)	2,000 (67%)	3,000 (60%)
Not Effective	3,000 (60%)	2,000 (67%)	1,000 (33%)	2,000 (40%)

74. *Simpson's paradox. Effectiveness of medication as reported by Doctors A and B, individually.*

According to Doctor A's study, the new drug is effective on 40 percent of the men but only on 33 percent of the women. Doctor B's study confirms Doctor A's conclusion, showing that the drug is effective on 67 percent of the men but only on 60 percent of the women. Yet, when the statistics are combined, as shown in Figure 75, the results are quite different.

Of course, another set of data, such as those presented in Figure 76, could completely reverse the outcome. Here we see that in Doctor A's study the drug is effective on 43 percent of the men but on only 33 percent of the women, whereas in Doctor B's study the

Effectiveness of Medication	Combined Results	
	Men	Women
Effective	4,000 (50%)	4,000 (50%)
Not Effective	4,000 (50%)	4,000 (50%)

75. *Simpson's paradox. Effectiveness of medication according to the combined results of Doctors A and B.*

Effectiveness of Medication	Doctor A's Results		Doctor B's Results		Combined Results	
	Men	Women	Men	Women	Men	Women
Effective	300 (43%)	100 (33%)	400 (67%)	700 (64%)	700 (54%)	800 (57%)
Not Effective	400 (57%)	200 (67%)	200 (33%)	400 (36%)	600 (46%)	600 (43%)

76. *Simpson's paradox. Another example of reversed results caused by combined data.*

drug is effective on 67 percent of the men but on only 64 percent of the women. Yet when combined, the statistics show the drug to be effective on 57 percent of the women but on only 54 percent of the men. The results of the effectiveness of the new drug have been reversed.

While the examples above are hypothetical in order to clarify the explanation of the principles involved, real-world examples of Simpson's paradox have been found in statistical studies. For example, several independent studies showed that in the 1970s there was bias against female candidates for graduate school admissions on the Berkeley campus of the University of California, but when the statistics were combined the bias was slightly against the men. Similarly, studies have shown that it is possible to conclude on the basis of several different observations that Runner A is likely to win in a race against Runner B, but the opposite may be demonstrated by the combined statistics.

It is also possible that data will provide support for each of two different conclusions and disconfirm the conjunction of the two conclusions. Consider, for example, this somewhat fanciful, though plausible, situation. A man wishes to buy a car that is both luxuriously comfortable and economical to drive. Some of the cars the buyer is familiar with are American-made and others are European-made. Being a wise consumer, the man decides to test drive several cars of each type. In two weeks he drives five different American cars and five different European cars, and he concludes that 3/5 (60 percent) of the American-made cars are luxuriously comfortable but that only 2/5 (40 percent) of the European-made cars fulfill his comfort requirements. The man also determines on the basis of his trial tests that 3/5 (60 percent) of the American-made cars but only 2/5 (40 percent) of the European-made cars are economical.

One would suppose the man to be reasonable in concluding that he should buy an American-made car if he wishes to maximize the possibility of getting a vehicle that is both luxuriously comfortable and economical to drive. However, this depends on the distribution of attributes among the two types of cars. Consider, for example, the data presented in Figure 77.

	COMFORTABLE	ECONOMICAL
American Car 1	+	+
American Car 2	−	+
American Car 3	−	+
American Car 4	+	−
American Car 5	+	−
European Car 1	+	+
European Car 2	+	+
European Car 3	−	−
European Car 4	−	−
European Car 5	−	−

77. *The test-drive paradox.*

The man's test results clearly show that the attribute of being luxuriously comfortable is found more frequently among American-made cars than among European-made cars, as is the attribute of being economical. However, there is only one American-made car tested that has *both* attributes, whereas there are two European-made cars with both attributes. Thus, the conjunction of the two desired characteristics is found more frequently among European-made cars despite the fact that taken separately each individual attribute occurs more frequently among the American-made cars. The conclusion to be drawn here is quite clear: when dealing with statistics, as with cars, *caveat emptor*.

See also PROBABILITY PARADOXES and THE PARADOX OF VOTING.

TIME PARADOXES

In Steven Spielberg's film *Close Encounters of the Third Kind,* shortly after the aliens land on Devil's Tower, they set free some Air Force pilots whom they had taken captive about forty years earlier. The men are still dressed in their Air Force uniforms. A ground technician who has assisted in the landing comments, "They haven't aged. Einstein was right." The reference is to the best-known paradox of modern physics—the twin paradox—which results from Albert Einstein's special theory of relativity.

Imagine that twins here on earth—let's call them Peter and Paul —synchronize their watches at 8:00 A.M. on January 1, 2000. Peter then leaves the house and boards a spaceship. He takes off on a long, high-speed journey through the solar system. Meanwhile, Paul stays at home and takes care of the family business. When Peter returns home, the twins check their watches, which show different times. Whose watch will show the earlier time?

The special theory of relativity forces us to conclude that Peter's watch, like the captured Air Force pilots' watches, is sure to record an earlier time than Paul's. The difference in the time shown by the two watches might amount to several hours or to several million years, depending on how fast (and how far) the spaceship travels. The closer the spaceship comes to traveling at the speed of light, the greater the difference in the clocks. This paradoxical phenomenon, called "time dilation," occurs because as the velocity of an object or a person increases, time "slows down." In fact, if Peter traveled *at* the speed of light, no time at all would elapse for him, and

Paul would probably be long since dead and buried when Peter returns to earth.

For us to understand the twin paradox better, it helps to examine some of the problems that Einstein was considering when he formulated his special theory of relativity.

Imagine that the twins are both here on earth. Peter gets in his car and travels at a uniform speed of 50 miles per hour. Paul follows in his car at a somewhat slower speed of 40 miles per hour. Newtonian physics tells us that Peter's car is moving away from Paul's at a velocity of 10 miles per hour, the difference in the speed of the two cars. Similarly, if Peter and Paul were approaching each other in their cars, each traveling at 50 miles an hour, then the speed of each car relative to the other car is the sum of the two velocities, or one hundred miles per hour.

Common sense leads us to conclude that what is true of the cars should also be true of the light beams coming from their headlights. Yet, an important experiment by the American scientists Albert Michelson and Edward Morley in 1887 demonstrated conclusively that regardless of the velocity at which Peter or Paul might travel, each will always measure the velocity of light relative to him to be 299,800 kilometers per second. At the time Einstein was working on his special theory of relativity (which was published in 1905), the results of the Michelson-Morley experiment were considered a genuine paradox, for the experimental data seemed to contradict fundamental laws of Newtonian mechanics.

Einstein opened the way to his extraordinary solution by accepting the experimental data as true rather than faulty. Thus, the first postulate of special relativity is that the velocity of light as it moves through a vacuum is constant for all observers who move uniformly relative to the source of the light. Einstein's second postulate was really an extension of Newton's principle of relativity. Newton's laws show that an observer on a uniformly moving object (for example, a car or a plane) who has no way of seeing the "outside" world cannot possibly determine if it is he who is moving or the world outside. Einstein concluded that the cause of the constancy of the velocity of light had something to do with the means by which it is measured. In other words, as we shift our frame of reference, there must be a change in the instruments—the clock and the ruler—by which we measure the velocity of light.

Einstein distinguished between proper and relative time and proper and relative length and indicated that these are more accurately considered local properties. For example, all of us observers on earth share the same proper time and length. Those observers in other frames of reference—for example, within a speeding spaceship—also have their own proper time and length. Our observations of their moving clock and ruler involve relative time and length, as do their observations of our clock and ruler. Proper time and proper length never appear to vary to the observers in the same frame of reference, whereas relative time is always slower than proper time and relative length is always shorter than proper length.

Thus, for Peter time passes normally on his ship regardless of its speed, whereas Paul "sees" Peter's clock slowing down and his ruler contracting. Likewise, for Peter, it is Paul who is moving at fast speeds, and thus it is Paul's clock that is slowing down and his ruler that is contracting. Once we have distinctions for proper and relative time and length, it is possible to account for the counterintuitive time characteristics involved in the twin paradox.

For example, let us assume that Peter is in a stationary spaceship. On the ceiling of the main control room is a light bulb and below it on the floor is a light-sensitive detector attached to a stopwatch. At a certain moment, Peter touches a button, the light is flashed from the bulb and the stopwatch starts ticking. When the light strikes the light detector, the stopwatch stops. Assuming that the control room is 3 meters tall, it will take about 10 nanoseconds for the light to reach the detector—at least, this is the time elapsed according to Peter's measurement.

Now, let us suppose that Paul is in another spaceship traveling past Peter's ship at a constant velocity v. What will Peter observe? First, let us not forget that for Paul it is as if Peter's ship is moving and his own ship is stationary. Suppose that at the moment Peter sets off the flash, Paul's stopwatch with light detector also starts to measure the passage of time. (Figure 78A). As time passes, Paul finds himself in the position shown in Figure 78B. Notice that the light in Peter's ship is traveling downward but has not yet reached Peter's light-sensitive stopwatch. Finally, the light strikes Peter's stopwatch and, thereby, also stops Paul's clock at some point when Paul's spaceship passes under Peter's (Figure 78C).

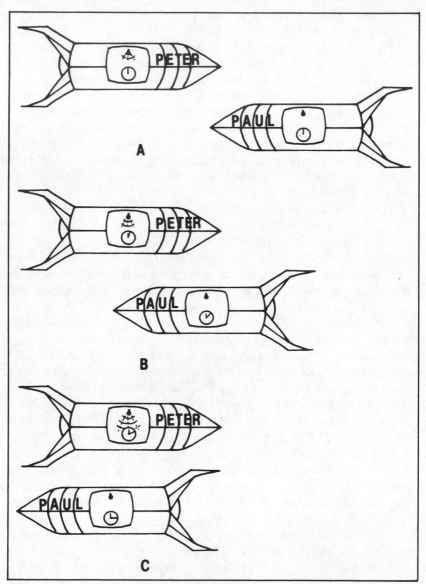

78. The paradox of the twins.

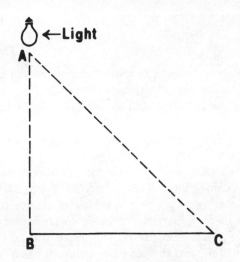

79. *The diagonal direction of the light velocity observed by Paul.*

As diagramed in Figure 79, for Peter the velocity of light is measured as a vertical line from point *A* to point *B* (ceiling to floor), whereas for Paul it is measured as a diagonal line from point *A* to point *C*. It is obvious that *AB* is a shorter distance than *AC*, yet we know that the velocity of light is constant. Whereas Peter measures the time that has passed as 10 nanoseconds, Paul, who let us assume is traveling at a velocity of 60 percent of the speed of light, will observe Peter's clock as having measured 12.5 nanoseconds, a time dilation of 25 percent. Of course, the relationship is perfectly symmetrical. Paul observes that his own watch has measured 10 nanoseconds, but Peter's observation of Paul's watch shows that 12.5 nanoseconds have passed.

Implicit in the phenomenon of time dilation is the fact that while observers within the same frame of reference can talk about an event happening *now*, *before*, or *after*, these terms will not necessarily agree with the observation of the same event seen by another observer in a different frame of reference. It is possible for Observer A to see events *X* and *Y* as occurring simultaneously, whereas Observer B, who is moving in a different frame of reference, will see event *X* occur *before* event *Y*.

Time dilation is not something that happens just in theory. Many experimental tests have supported Einstein's conclusions that time slows down as velocity increases and that an object contracts in the direction of its acceleration. For example, in 1971 four atomic clocks were flown around the world, first eastward and then westward. When the atomic clocks were compared to the control ones on the ground, they were found to be out of step with their ground counterparts, even though they had all been synchronized before the experiment. The differences were exactly those predicted by relativity theory.

Other experiments dealing with the acceleration of subatomic particles have consistently shown that the average lifetime of such particles increases as their velocity increases. As we measure the average lifetime of these particles, they seem from our perspective to live longer the faster they move, but from the perspective of the particles, their lifetime is the same regardless of their velocities.

Moving at high velocities will cause time from the mover's viewpoint to slow down, and if a person achieved the speed of light, time for him would stop completely. What might we expect to happen if we exceeded the speed of light? Hypothetical faster-than-light particles called "tachyons" were postulated by physicists soon after Einstein's theory of relativity was first published. In 1917 the American physicist Richard C. Tolman presented an argument which demonstrated that if faster-than-light signals could be propagated, then communication with the past would be possible; such signals would, in effect, comprise a "tachyonic antitelephone," as later researchers called it. Assuming a modulated tachyonic signal beam, proper equipment, and two communicators, here is how it would work:

Imagine that Mr. Hindsyte buys the evening paper on his way home and notices that Paradox Industries jumped 20 points in late afternoon stock market trading. When Hindsyte gets home, he immediately goes to his tachyonic antitelephone and calls his stockbroker, Mr. Foresyte, of Sybil Seer & Foresyte, and reaches him at noon of that same day. "Foresyte, this is Hindsyte," he says. "Listen, I want you to sell everything I have and put it all into Paradox Industries, and move quickly—before one o'clock." Foresyte does move quickly on Hindsyte's request, and Hindsyte makes a small fortune.

Meanwhile, Foresyte uses Hindsyte's information to his own benefit and to the benefit of a few key clients. He calls each of them on his tachyonic antitelephone and delivers his hot tip early that morning. In his excitement Foresyte accidentally calls Hindsyte at 9:00 A.M. the same day and blurts out the suggestion to buy

Paradox Industries before one o'clock that afternoon. Something very curious is happening here, for how can Hindsyte receive the information as a tip nine hours before he gives it to Foresyte?

The backward-in-time communication made possible by the tachyonic antitelephone can produce powerful causal contradictions such as the one presented above. However, the paradoxes here are multiple. Consider, for example, the fact that if Hindsyte receives the information as a tip from Foresyte, then Hindsyte would have no cause to call Foresyte at six o'clock that evening; but without the call from Hindsyte, Foresyte would be without the information and so would not call Hindsyte at nine o'clock that morning, and so on.

The paradox can be made more evident by the following example. Imagine that Hindsyte and Foresyte enter into the following agreement: Hindsyte will send a message at six o'clock that evening if and only if he does not receive a message at one o'clock. Foresyte sends a message to Hindsyte at one o'clock immediately upon receiving one from Hindsyte at three o'clock that afternoon. In this case, the exchange of messages will take place if and only if it does not take place (Figure 80).

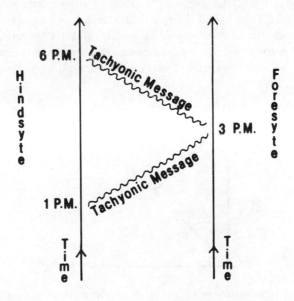

80. The tachyonic antitelephone paradox.

Although a number of experiments have attempted to prove the existence of tachyons, to date none has done so. However, this itself may be viewed paradoxically, since researchers have concluded that faster-than-light tachyonic communications would necessarily involve a reversal of normal "if-then" causality to "then-if" causality. In other words, the experimental results would always precede the experiment; the answer would always arrive before the question had been asked. As with the communication between Hindsyte and Foresyte, for tachyonic experiments to be successful, they must fail —which has been the case so far.

Although faster-than-light particles have yet to be discovered, time-reversed events have been "observed" on the particle level according to quantum field theory. In 1949 Nobel laureate Richard Feynman, an American physicist, demonstrated that the mathematical formula for a positron field propagating forward in time is exactly the same as an electron field propagating backward in time. In other words, Feynman proved that it is not only possible, but in some cases preferable, to view an antiparticle as a particle traveling backward in time.

Figure 81 presents a very simple space-time diagram, one that represents an electron emitting a photon. In the subatomic world, all happenings are called "events." Subatomic events always involve the annihilation of the original particles and the creation of new ones. In Figure 81, the solid line at the lower left indicates an electron as it moves through space with a certain velocity. The dot

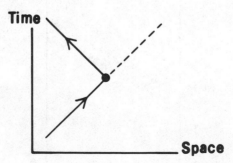

81. Feynman space-time diagram of an electron emitting a photon.

indicates the point in time and space when the event (the electron emitting the photon) takes place. The photon (represented by the dotted line) flies off to the right at the speed of light. Meanwhile, the course of the electron is altered by the emission of the photon, and the electron moves off to the left, though with somewhat slower momentum than it had before.

It is possible to use similar diagrams to represent more complex subatomic events. For instance, Figure 82 shows a space-time diagram of two subatomic events. First, there is a collision between two photons at point B, which creates an electron-positron pair. Then, at A, an electron and a positron collide and create two photons. In this diagram, an arrowhead pointing upward indicates a particle (the electron) and an arrowhead pointing downward indicates an antiparticle (positron).

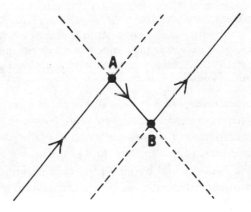

82. Feynman space-time diagram of two subatomic events.

The American physicist Gary Zukav notes in his book *The Dancing Wu Li Masters:*

> Ordinarily we would interpret these events as follows: Two photons collide in the lower right of the diagram producing an electron-positron pair. The electron flies off to the left where it meets another electron which has entered the diagram from the lower left. There they mutually annihilate and create two photons which depart in opposite directions.

The preferred interpretation of quantum field theory, however, is much simpler. In it there is only *one* particle. That particle, an electron, enters the diagram from the lower left and travels forward in time and space until it emits two photons at A. This causes it to reverse its direction in time. Traveling backward in time as a positron it absorbs two photons at B, reverses direction in time again, and again becomes an electron. Instead of three particles there is only one particle which, moving from left to right, travels first forward in time, then backward in time, and then forward in time again.

A space-time diagram should not be viewed as a chronology of subatomic events, but rather as a representation of subatomic events which, when viewed from the perspective of four dimensions, is "timeless." As the French physicist Louis de Broglie noted:

> In space-time, everything which for each of us constitutes the past, the present, and the future is given *en bloc*. . . . Each observer, as his time passes, discovers, so to speak, new slices of space-time which appear to him as successive aspects of the material world, though in reality the ensemble of events constituting space-time exist prior to his knowledge of them.

All that we are dealing with here is one way to interpret a Feynman diagram that represents certain subatomic events. This is not the only interpretation, and it does not mean that the physical particles actually reverse in time. All that the Feynman diagram is really saying is that the field created by an antiparticle moving forward in time is the same mathematically as the field created by a particle moving backward in time.

Although subatomic particles can be viewed as reversing their time direction, a molecule or anything larger is prevented from doing so by the second law of thermodynamics. Time appears to be related to and to flow in the direction of entropy, the tendency of all physical systems to go from order to disorder. Time-reversed events—such as a mixture of tea and sugar separating upon being stirred—are possible, though extremely improbable. The laws of probability prevent us from successfully engaging in such time-reversals, but the laws of relativity make it theoretically possible for us to travel into the future.

See also THE GRUE-BLEEN PARADOX.

TOPOLOGICAL PARADOXES

If you take a strip of paper, 2 inches by 14 inches, and paste its narrow ends as shown in Figure 83, you would form a band. This band has two edges, one upper and one lower, and two surfaces or planes, one interior and one exterior. Now, if you take an identical strip of paper, but before the ends are pasted give it a half twist, how many edges and surfaces will this band have?

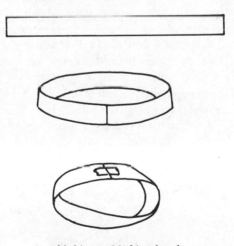

83. Making a Möbius band.

It seems reasonable to conclude that the twisted band, known as a "Möbius band," also has two edges and two surfaces. However, two simple experiments are sure to illuminate the paradoxical properties of this topological curiosity. Begin by constructing a Möbius band from a strip of plain paper with the dimensions mentioned above.

Then take a colored pencil or crayon and begin to color one side of the Möbius band without lifting the pencil or crayon from the paper. Continue in this manner—until you realize that you have colored the entire surface of the Möbius band, because it has only one surface.

Now place the Möbius band on a table and put a finger on the highest edge of the figure. Then place a finger of your other hand on the lower surface, directly opposite the upper finger. Keep the upper finger stationary as you move the lower finger along the "lower" edge—and you run smack into your other finger on the "upper" edge. The Möbius band, as this experiment demonstrates, has only one edge, which befits a figure with only one surface. Somehow, the half twist causes the figure to gobble up one of its own surfaces and one of its own edges.

The amazing properties of such simple bands were unknown until one was described in the mid-nineteenth century by the German astronomer and mathematician August Ferdinand Möbius. The study of such one-surface figures now constitutes an area of topology. Further experimentation with Möbius bands produces other paradoxical effects. For example, if you draw a line down the middle of the Möbius band and then cut it along the line, as shown in Figure 84, you probably would expect two bands; but you would, in fact, end up with one single larger band. If you examine this new band carefully, you will determine that it has four twists in it as well as two surfaces and two edges. It is not a Möbius band; furthermore, if you bisect *this* band as you had the Möbius band, you will get not one larger band but two interlocking bands.

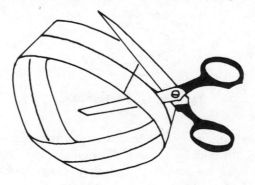

84. Cutting a Möbius band.

The geometry of this phenomenon is not difficult to grasp. Any figure with an odd number of half twists is a Möbius band in the sense that it is a topological object with one surface and one edge. For example, a Möbius band with three half twists, when cut down the middle, would produce only one larger band, but with eight half twists. (To calculate the number of half twists that will be produced by bisecting a Möbius band, simply double the number of half twists in the band and add two.)

Any Möbius band that is bisected produces a non-Möbius band; that is, a band with two surfaces and two edges—and always with an even number of half twists. When a band with an even number of half twists is bisected, two bands result, each with the same number of half twists as the original but knotted together with half as many links as the number of half twists. Thus if we bisected a band with eight half twists, we would produce two bands, each with eight half twists but knotted together with four links.

When we make a Möbius band by giving the strip of paper a half twist, we join the ends so that they have opposite orientations. If a two-dimensional creature (for example, a creature like those in Edwin Abbott's *Flatland*) who lives in the plane of the Möbius band travels around the band, then when he returns to his starting point he will be a mirror-image of himself at the starting point.

The paradoxical qualities of Möbius bands can be made more startling by constructing a double Möbius band; that is, placing two strips of paper of equal dimensions together and then giving them the required half twist (Figure 85). At first, it would seem that what has been created is a pair of nested Möbius bands. This can be tested by slipping a toothpick or matchstick between the bands so that the ends of the object stick out on either side and then by moving the toothpick or matchstick around between the bands until it returns to the starting point. It is clear that we are dealing with two bands, for there is always a space between them.

Yet, if you try to re-create the crayon experiment performed on the original single Möbius band and start at the bottom on the outside lower band, you will find that your crayon when you return to the starting point is above it on the inside upper band. If you continue with the crayon experiment, you will return to your exact starting point having twice circumnavigated the double Möbius

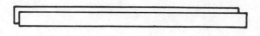

85. Making a double Möbius band. Take two sheets of plain paper and cut identical strips about 14″ × 1″. Keeping the strips together as shown; give them a half twist; then connect the ends on each side with a piece of tape. (Make sure you don't tape the two bands to each other.)

band. Thus, the two bands are not nested, as our first experiment seemed to prove, but rather they are one band with one surface and one edge. You can prove this by pulling the bands apart and discovering one large Möbius band with four half twists!

Figure 86 shows a wood engraving made by the Dutch graphic artist M. C. Escher in 1963. Even though pairs of ants appear to be opposite each other, they all exist on the same plane since the Möbius band has only one surface. Escher's use of ants hints at a famous Victorian version of the paradox, which described an ant walking around the entire surface of the Möbius band without crossing from one side to another.

Topologists consider the Möbius band a "non-orientable surface." As defined by the German mathematicians David Hilbert and Stephan Cohn-Vossen, "A surface is non-orientable if and only if there exists on the surface some closed curve . . . such that a small oriented circle whose center traverses the curve continuously will arrive at its starting point with its orientation reversed."

Another topological paradox that has a closed non-orientable surface is the Klein bottle, named after the German mathematician Felix Klein, who began the modern synthesis of geometry in the late nineteenth century. It is important to know at the outset that the Klein bottle is a two-dimensional figure; it cannot be constructed in three-dimensional space without intersecting its own surfaces, although a "perfect" four-dimensional model is theoretically possible. As you see in Figure 87 the "neck" of the Klein bottle bends around and enters the bottle and there fuses with the

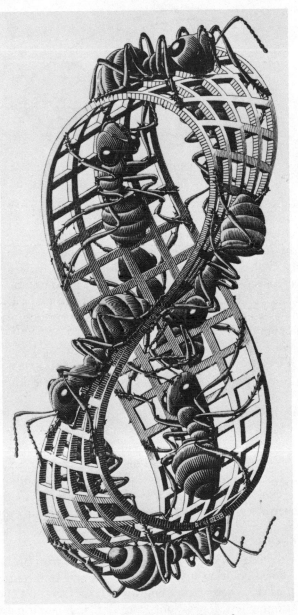

86. Möbius Strip, II, *by M. C. Escher*.

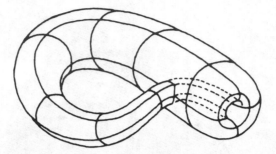

87. The Klein bottle.

other open end, forming one smooth continuous surface. In a three-dimensional model, there would be a hole where the neck passes through the side of the bottle. But the Klein bottle is only a two-dimensional figure. In fact, the bottle has no hole where the neck and side intersect—the surface of the bottle is continuous; that is, the inside surface is continuous with the outside (as with the two "apparent" sides of a Möbius band) and this surface also covers what appears to be the hole.

As Martin Gardner, creator of the "Mathematical Games" column in *Scientific American,* notes in a fascinating article called "Klein Bottles and Other Surfaces," the Klein bottle exhibits several paradoxical qualities, among them the fact that it is a one-sided figure with no inside, no outside, and no edge. Interested readers will find that Gardner's article presents simple plans (originally devised by science-fiction writer Stephan Barr) for constructing a paper model of the Klein bottle. This model has only one flaw: it contains a slot where the planes intersect, corresponding to the "hole" that would occur in a three-dimensional glass model of the bottle. Nevertheless, constructing the paper model and experimenting with it do make the paradoxical characteristics of the Klein bottle and its relation to the Möbius band evident.

Another topological curiosity is the four-color map problem. It is customary when coloring maps or globes to give different colors to two countries that share a common boundary. Based on the experience of cartographers, it was long considered an empirical fact that no more than four colors were necessary to color any map or

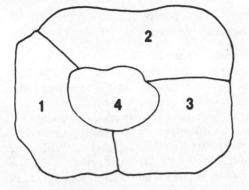

88. The four-color map problem.

globe. Figure 88 shows a simple map of four countries, each of which shares boundaries with the other three. It cannot be colored correctly with fewer than four colors.

The origins of the four-color map problem can be traced to a related problem posed by Möbius to his students in 1840. Despite several attempts by noted nineteenth-century mathematicians, no one was able to prove mathematically that only four colors suffice. The best that anyone could demonstrate was that five colors will suffice. For more than a hundred years, mathematics was unable to resolve the problem that reality clearly posed.

It was not until 1977 that three American mathematicians—Kenneth Appel, Wolfgang Haken, and John Koch—with the aid of high-speed computer technology, published a "proof" which has been thoroughly reviewed and is now generally accepted by most mathematicians. However, this new proof for what is now called the "four-color theorem" has been challenged by some mathematicians on philosophical grounds.

Consider, for example, the argument presented by the American Thomas Tymoczko in a 1979 article in the *Journal of Philosophy*. Tymoczko argues that if we accept the work of Appel, Haken, and Koch, we must be willing to alter radically our traditional views of mathematics. According to Tymoczko, the proof for the four-color theorem hinges on the use of a computer to examine over a thousand subcases "most of which cannot be handled except by high-speed computers." We accept the proof even though mathematicians are unable to survey the proof. As Tymoczko notes,

> Mathematicians cannot work out the missing steps for themselves, not even in a lifetime of work; and it is nowhere recorded in the archives. What is recorded is the evidence that a computer once worked out the missing steps. So it would be a grave mistake to classify the appeal to computers as a theoretically dispensable convenience, like the appeal to published journal articles. Of course the appeal "by computer" does mark an abbreviation. . . . The point at hand, however, is that surveyability is preserved in traditional descriptions of proofs, but not in the appeal to computers.

Tymoczko maintains that although a mathematical solution to the four-color problem has been achieved, a new four-color problem has arisen. It would seem that accepting the four-color theorem forces mathematicians and philosophers to change their concept of the nature of mathematical proof. It requires that empirical evidence from experiments such as the computer programs in the Appel, Haken, and Koch work be included in the notion of proof. Until the advent of the four-color theorem and other computer-assisted proofs, the deductive nature of mathematical proof was considered to be the paradigm of mathematical thought.

See also GEOMETRIC VANISHES.

THE UNEXPECTED EXAMINATION PARADOX

A professor of logic named Pico announced one Friday that on one day of the following week he would give his students an unexpected examination. According to the professor, who was known to be a truthful man, the students would have no way of knowing which was to be the day of the examination until they walked into the classroom and it was announced. After the class was dismissed, several students walked to the student union, where the following discussion took place.

"Can you imagine what's gotten into old Pico? 'One day next week I will give you an unexpected examination. Let me specify the conditions of this examination—'" said Chris, mocking Professor Pico's precise intonations.

"What's the difference if we do know when we're going to get it?" said Joe. "Nobody here is likely to pass it anyway; that is, no one except for Danielle—"

"I'm not so sure there will be a test," responded Danielle.

"Are you crazy?" said Chris. "You heard the man yourself. He said, 'One day—'"

"I know what he said. I heard him too," said Danielle sharply. "But why don't you *think* about what he said."

"Go on, then," prodded Joe.

"Well, he said that we wouldn't know about the exam until we got to class that day. In that case, he can't give us the exam on Friday because by class time Thursday, when we still hadn't received the examination, we would know that he was giving it to us the next day, right?"

"Right. But so what? We know the test won't be on Friday, but there's still Monday through Thursday," said Chris.

"Yes," said Danielle with a slight edge of triumph in her voice, "but the same argument holds true for Thursday. Don't you see? We know it won't be Friday. Likewise, by Wednesday's class if we hadn't yet received the examination, we would know that we were getting it on Thursday, so we can't get it on Thursday either. The same is true for Wednesday, and Tuesday—"

"So we know we are getting it on Monday, right?" stated Chris with confidence.

"That's just the half of it. We now know that Pico can't give us the test Monday without contradicting his word that we wouldn't know the day of the test in advance. So you see, he can't give us the test at all," exclaimed Danielle.

"A lot of good that will do us on Monday when he hands us the test," said Chris.

"Well, I don't know about you, but I'm going to Pico's office now to call his bluff. Anyone care to join me?" asked Danielle.

The students caught Pico just as he was locking his office door and getting ready to leave for the weekend. Danielle was the spokesperson for the group. After explaining her argument, Professor Pico just smiled and said, "Well, I'm glad to see you're thinking." Then he walked away.

The students didn't know quite what to make of Pico's remarks. When Monday's class arrived and the professor handed out no test booklets, Danielle and her supporters felt great relief. No test was given on Tuesday either. On Wednesday, the professor told the students to put away their books and get ready to take the unexpected examination he had told them about last Friday. Has the professor violated his word? What, if anything, was wrong with Danielle's reasoning?

Quite obviously, the good Professor Pico has not violated his word. The examination was totally unexpected when he gave it; that is, the students did not know the day of the examination until they arrived in class. However, the logical problems generated by the unexpected examination are much more complex.

The origin of this paradox has been traced to a broadcast made by the Swedish Radio Service during World War II. The original announcement involved a civil defense exercise which was to take place one day the following week; but in order to make certain that the units were truly prepared, no one was to know in advance which day the exercise would occur. The paradoxical characteristics of the announcement were noticed by Lennart Ekbom, a Swedish professor of mathematics, who discussed the problem with his students. It first appeared in print in a 1948 issue of the British logic journal *Mind*.

In order to understand the complexities of the argument it is necessary to identify and examine the statements that comprise it. Returning to our unexpected examination version, the professor's two statements—"There will be an examination on some school day next week" and "The students will not know the date of the examination before the examination actually takes place"—are premises of the argument. As the Scottish logician Thomas O'Beirne notes in a 1965 article on the paradox, there is a hidden assumption here that may be stated as, "The students may consider the professor's two statements as unconditionally true."

If we accept the first statement as true, then it is reasonable to conclude that if Friday arrives without there having been an examination earlier in the week, there must be an examination on Friday. However, the truth of the third statement (the hidden assumption that the first two statements must be true) implies that the students would have to know by the end of the day Thursday that there would be an exam the next day. Of course, if we accept the second statement as true, then it is impossible for the students to expect the examination at any time. The contradiction initially is avoided by concluding that Friday cannot arrive without the examination having taken place already. As we saw, this approach provides only a temporary solution: eventually we prove that the examination could not have taken place (logically) within the time during which it must take place—at least, if we accept the first premise as true.

According to O'Beirne, the paradox arises by considering all *three* statements—including the one that asserts the truth of the first two—as being unconditionally true. In fact, all three premises cannot be true; at least one must be false or, as we have seen, we are lead to draw contradictory conclusions. As O'Beirne notes,

> This means that *if* our first two statements *are* true, it becomes *logically absurd* to assume that the pupils—in any way whatever— could properly be *convinced* that both were true: for *this* is what

leads to the contradiction. *Truth* of the two statements and justification of the right of the pupils to *assume* their truth, are two entirely different matters; and if the first two statements *are in fact* true, this very fact—logically and automatically—must *prohibit* the pupils from *assuming* that they are true.

Now we can easily verify that the first two statements can be true, but only if the third statement is false. Thus, the teacher can give an examination on any day, even Friday, but the students cannot logically expect it. Once the examination has been given, then the first two statements must be true (this will be obvious in retrospect), but it cannot be demonstrated to be the case in advance. Of course, it is advance knowledge of the truth of the statements which is needed in order to prove that the teacher lied in his announcement of the unexpected examination.

In summary, O'Beirne argues that a statement about a future event can be known to be true by one person (in this case the professor) and not known to be true by the other parties (the students) until after the event has taken place. The implications of this fact for the resolution of the paradox were made clear by Michael Scriven, a professor of logic and philosophy at the Indiana University, in another version of the paradox which involves two boxes and an unexpected egg.

Imagine two boxes numbered 1 and 2 and placed on a desk. You are told by your friend that in one of the boxes there exists an unexpected egg. The boxes can be opened only in sequence, Box 1 first and Box 2 second. You are asked to determine which box contains the unexpected egg. Scriven then specifies what an "unexpected egg" means. He notes that it cannot be considered totally unexpected since we were told that there is an egg in one of the two boxes. Furthermore, if we opened Box 1 and found it empty, then there would be nothing unexpected in the fact that the egg is in Box 2.

Based on this, you are likely to conclude that the egg must be in Box 1; however, if it *must* be in Box 1, it is no longer unexpected. It seems as if there cannot be an unexpected egg at all! Yet, the matter is not quite so simple, for your friend claims that there *is* an egg in one of the boxes and the fact is there is nothing you can do to argue it away logically. Furthermore, by not being able to decide on the location of the egg, it continues to remain unexpected.

In a 1951 article published in *Mind* magazine, Scriven continues with the following argument:

> If the egg is not in box one, we should know before opening the second lid that it was in box two, and it would not be unexpected. So the only possibility which might make you right, is that the egg is in box one. Yet since we shall expect to find the egg there, it will not be unexpected; in fact, the egg cannot be unexpected, so you are wrong. We do *not* have to show in which box the egg reposes in order to show that it is not unexpected, but only that it cannot be in either and be unexpected. We were puzzled at first because it seemed the egg had some magic property that caused it to vanish whenever we had deduced its whereabouts. But now you tell us that there is a real egg in one of the boxes and you go on wrongly to claim that it will not be unexpected. True, it may be expected wrongly, but only if your own statement was wrong. There is something very queer about the statement "There is an unexpected egg in one box." It suggests, or can be taken to suggest, one state of affairs: the presence of a special kind of egg. But we find that this isn't a special kind of egg in the way that speckled, double yolked, or Easter eggs are special. Not at all: unexpected eggs, for one thing, may be expected at the same time (with respect to the conditions of some other problem and problem-solver). Yet the argument proceeds as though they were eggs with some observable peculiarity, and when (on that assumption) we have deduced their whereabouts, the prize is magically spirited away. The argument, which works so well with addled or ostrich eggs whose presence is asserted in one of the boxes, will not do for unexpected eggs (or, if you like, the assertion won't do), because neither of the possible alternatives, (1) there must be an unexpected egg in box one, or (2) there must be an unexpected egg in box two, is sensible if the unexpectedness applies to the person to whom the alternatives are presented. Since these statements are not themselves sensible, it is not sensible to talk of ruling them out. Nor sensible to make a statement which is the equivalent to a disjunction of such alternatives.

In fact, what has happened here is that we are caught in an endless round of vicious circularity and contradiction. At first, we assume that the other person's statement that the egg will be unexpected is true. From this we deduce that the egg is in Box 1; but if it is in Box 1, the other person's statement about the unexpectedness of the egg is false. If this statement is false, then we have no reason to infer that the egg is in Box 1; and if we can't infer this, then the man's statement about the unexpectedness of the egg is true!

Even if we open Box 1 and there is no egg in it, can we deduce conclusively that the egg will be in Box 2? Unfortunately not, for if we assume that there is an egg in Box 2 and there is, then it is not unexpected as we had been told and so the other person has spoken falsely. However, if we also assume that the other person spoke truly about the unexpectedness of the egg, then there can't be an egg in Box 2. To paraphrase the noted logician Willard V. Quine, who discussed another variation of this paradox, it is important to distinguish the four possibilities that exist for the person determining the location of the egg: (1) There is an egg in Box 2 and I know it now; (2) There is no egg in Box 2 and I know it now; (3) There is no egg in Box 2 and I do not know it now; and (4) There is an egg in Box 2 and I do not know it now. Since I do not know either of the first two cases to be true, they can be eliminated as possibilities. The last two cases are open possibilities, and the very last would fulfill the conditions specified by the person who put the egg in the box. He knows, as does the professor, that his prediction of the unexpectedness of the event is logically sound, but the other parties in these situations cannot know that; and, hence, they cannot use his prediction as the premise of an argument which concludes that the prediction itself is unsound.

Other commentators have found flaws in Quine's reasoning, arguing that if the problem is formulated more precisely—for example, if the professor says "There will be an examination on one of the next n days, and it will be impossible to deduce in advance on which day the test will be given, using this announcement as a premise of your argument"—then Quine's distinctions apparently lose their force. Other approaches to the problem, including set theoretic and probabilistic ones, have also failed to provide a totally satisfactory solution to the paradox.

See also THE PREDICTION PARADOX.

VISUAL ILLUSIONS

A visual illusion is an optical experience that seems to contradict reality. Such a definition implicitly distinguishes between subjective experiences, of which visual perception is one, and the objectivity of the real world. A visual illusion, therefore, is often thought of as a "misreading" of the stimuli produced by certain objects or images.

Among the most common visual illusions are those that involve distortions produced by lines and angles. One such illusion, which frequently appears in children's books, is the top hat illusion shown in Figure 89. It seems as if the hat is taller than it is wide when, in fact, its height and width are the same. Similarly, line *CD* in Figure 90 seems longer than line *AB*, but in fact is the same length. These are both the same basic illusion. But what is it that causes this illusion?

89. The top hat illusion.

At first, researchers who studied this illusion believed that it was produced because the eyes moved more easily from side to side than they did upward and downward. This, however, is not really the case, as we can see in Figure 91. Here is the same illusion as shown in Figure 90, but this time the line *CD* is horizontal, and yet it still appears longer than line *AB*. The generally accepted explanation of the illusion claims that the brain tends to see the horizontal lines in the first two figures as shorter because they are interrupted by vertical lines. Similarly, the vertical line in Figure 91 seems shorter because it is interrupted by the horizontal line.

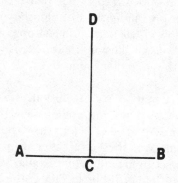

90. The interrupted horizontal line illusion.

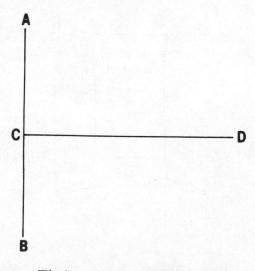

91. The interrupted vertical line illusion.

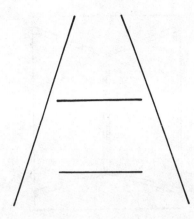

92. The Ponzo illusion.

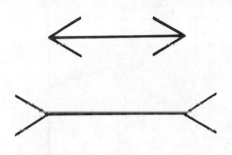

93. The Müller-Lyer illusion.

Somewhat related to the illusions in Figures 89, 90, and 91 are the well-known Ponzo and Müller-Lyer illusions shown in Figures 92 and 93, respectively. In the Ponzo illusion, named for the Italian psychologist Mario Ponzo, the top horizontal line is perceived as longer than the bottom horizontal line. In the Müller-Lyer illusion, named for Franz Müller-Lyer, the German psychiatrist, the line with the inward pointing arrowheads appears longer than the line with the outward pointing arrowheads.

According to the generally accepted theory, we misread the lengths of the lines involved because we cannot help but perceive them as representative of the three-dimensional world. This is true even though we know them to be two-dimensional and even though there is no background to distract or fool us. In both illusions we inappropriately scale or misread the lines in question. In-

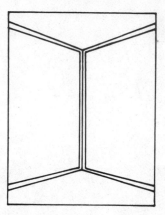

94. *The interior view of a corner.*

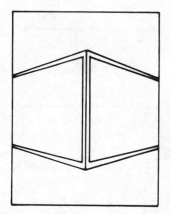

95. *The exterior view of a corner.*

deed, even when all depth information is removed from the illusions (through the elimination of stereoscopic viewing), they still are perceived as having depth (three dimensions) and the illusion persists.

It is generally believed that the persistence of such illusions is, perhaps, a function of our constant observations of similar—though not necessarily paradoxical—images. Notice, for example, that the interior and exterior views of a corner (Figures 94 and 95) produce the same effects as the Müller-Lyer illusion: when the floor and ceiling lines extend outward, the vertical line appears longer than when the floor and ceiling lines extend inward. When African tribe members, who were unfamiliar with square houses and three-dimensionally represented pictures, observed similar drawings, they did not perceive the illusions. To these people, the horizontal lines of the Ponzo and those of the Müller-Lyer illusion appeared to be the same size. Culture and constant visual reinforcement of the rules of central perspective make it impossible for Western eyes not to see differences in the lengths of these lines.

96. The Zöllner illusion.

Another optical illusion that involves distortion produced by lines and angles is the famous Zöllner parallel line illusion presented in Figure 96. Johann K. F. Zöllner, a German photometrist, first observed the illusion in a fabric pattern. If you look carefully at the drawing, it will seem that the vertical lines converge in the direction that the crossing lines diverge and vice versa. Thus, starting at the left, if you let your eyes scan the surface between the first two parallel lines moving from the top to the bottom of the picture, the two vertical lines will seem to grow farther apart. If you scan the area between the next two lines (moving from left to right) from bottom to top, you will observe the same phenomenon in the opposite direction. In fact, all the vertical lines are parallel. Similar distortions in parallel lines are produced in the Hering and Wundt il-

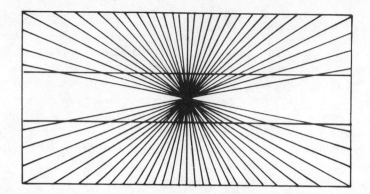

97. The Hering illusion.

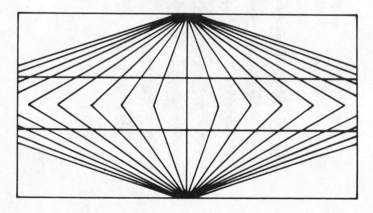

98. The Wundt illusion.

lusions, named, respectively, for the German psychologists Ewald Hering and Wilhelm Wundt, presented in Figures 97 and 98.

The context in which we observe an object or an image may produce an optical illusion by comparison or contrast. For example, in Figure 99 the circle that is closer to the vertex of the angle appears larger than the circle farther away. In fact, both circles are the same size. Similarly, although the central circles in both parts of Figure 100 are the same size, the circle surrounded by larger circles appears smaller than the circle that is surrounded by smaller circles. The illusions in both Figure 99 and Figure 100 are caused by the context in which we observe and compare and contrast the circles.

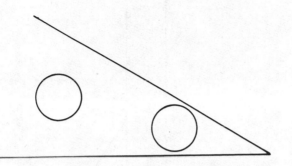

99. A comparison-contrast illusion, I.

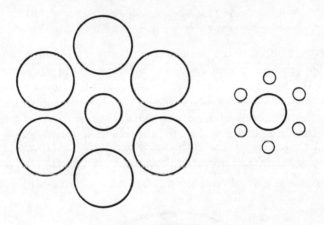

100. A comparison-contrast illusion, II.

A different though somewhat related distortion illusion is shown in Figure 101—first presented by the German physicist Johann Christoff Poggendorff. Here we see an oblique line intersecting a rectangular figure. The problem for the viewer is to determine which oblique line on the right is the natural continuation of the oblique line shown at the upper left of the rectangle. Viewed straight on, it would appear that the top oblique line on the right continues the line at the left. In fact, it is the bottom line. You can test this for yourself by placing the edge of a ruler or a piece of paper along the upper left line to see that it meets the lower right line. Unlike the illusions presented above, if you turn the Poggendorff figure so that the intersecting oblique line is either vertical or horizontal, then the illusion disappears.

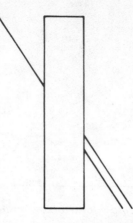

101. The Poggendorff illusion.

Distortion illusions are produced not only by straight lines and angles but also by circles and spirals. For example, if you trace a copy of the spiral shown in Figure 102 and place it on a turntable of a record player and spin the turntable in a counterclockwise direction, the spiral would appear to expand. Conversely, if the turntable is spun in a clockwise direction, it would appear to contract.

If you let the spiral spin either way for a few moments and then stop it with your hand, you will continue to see the spiral move, but in the opposite direction: an expanding spiral will suddenly

102. The expanding and contracting spiral illusion.

contract and vice versa. Furthermore, if you shift your eyes to another object, the object will appear to expand or shrink in the direction opposite to that of the spiral. Apparently, when viewing such a spiral the brain puts on "visual brakes." When the image is stopped suddenly, it takes a moment before the brain adjusts its counterspiral.

An irresistible set of visual illusions involving concentric circles was created by the British psychologist J. Frazier. Two of these are shown in Figures 103 and 104. In Figure 103 we see a twisted-cord spiral on a checkered background, and in Figure 104 we see twisted cords in the shape of television screens, also on a checkered background. What is amazing is that in both drawings the twisted cords actually form concentric circles. You can prove this by tracing some of the circles with a finger or with a pencil

103. The Frazier twisted-cord illusion, I.

104. The Frazier twisted-cord illusion, II.

and tracing paper. The illusion is produced by a combination of factors including the black and white twisting pattern of the cords and the way they intersect the background pattern. In the case of the spiral, the cords and checkered background force our eyes inward to the center of the print, thereby creating the illusion of a spiral which our brain finds irresistible.

Another type of visual illusion involves the influence of brightness and contrast on our perception. Consider, for example, the grid of black squares presented in Figure 105. If you stare at the grid for a few moments, you are sure to notice gray spots at the intersections of the white strips. Yet, if you stare at one of these gray spots directly, it will disappear and the surrounding gray spots will

105. The grid illusion.

grow darker. This phenomenon is probably caused by the fact that the contrast between the white and the black at the intersections is less than the contrast along the vertical and horizontal white strips. The greater the brightness contrast between two adjacent figures the whiter and larger the white will seem. Consequently, at the intersections where there is less contrast, we see the white as less white, or grayish, by comparison.

The background against which we see a figure or object will affect our perception of it. In Figure 106 the gray V on the black background appears lighter than the gray V on the white back-

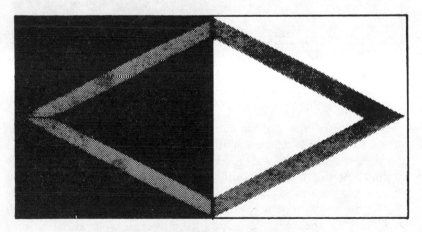

106. A brightness-contrast illusion.

ground. In fact, both V's are the same gray, the difference in their appearance being totally accounted for by the differences in contrast caused by the background.

The brightness and contrast of objects and images can also affect our perception of their size. The brighter the object, the larger it will appear. You can see this illusion at work in Figure 107, in which both squares are of identical size but the white one on the black background appears larger. This phenomenon is usually explained by the fact that a bright object more strongly stimulates the photoreceptors of the retina than a dim object. A bright light source excites not only the photoreceptors directly struck but also some of the adjacent photoreceptors, creating an image that spreads out and is, thus, enlarged a bit.

107. A size-perception contrast illusion.

Excitation of the rods and cones in the retina of the eye can create some paradoxical color illusions. For example, if you made a copy of the disk pictured in Figure 108 and spun it very quickly around a needle or pencil point, the black and white patterns on the disk would soon produce a color. The color would change depending on the speed at which you spin the disk. This visual illusion is produced by the red, blue, and green receptors in the retina of your eye, each of which has a different time constant. The pattern

108. The color disk illusion.

on the spinning disk stimulates these receptors at different intervals, thereby creating the sensation of color.

Lighting can also have an effect on our perceptions of concavity and convexity. A bas-relief illustration and an identical intaglio illustration can both be made to look convex when properly lighted. The photograph of the fossil in Figure 109 produces a similar illu-

109. The bas-relief–intaglio illusion.

sion: it would appear that the fossil is at the bottom and a mold made from it at the top. Yet, if we turn the picture upside down, the fossil and the mold seem to reverse positions. This illusion is due to the shifting shading of the radial lines of the fossil and mold as we change our view of them.

Not all visual illusions are man-made. Perhaps the most ancient and most discussed illusion in nature is the apparent difference in the size of the moon at the horizon and at its zenith in the sky. The moon at the horizon appears larger than it does at its zenith even though, in reality, it is farther away from the earth at the horizon and, hence, should be smaller. You can test this illusion for yourself. The next time you view a bright setting sun turn your eyes to the left or right, but keep them at the same plane as the sun. You will see an afterimage the same size as the sun. However, if you raise your eyes higher in the sky, the afterimage will appear considerably smaller than it did at the horizon. What accounts for this unexpected illusion?

Several theories have been offered to explain the moon illusion. According to one theory, the illusion occurs because we *expect* those objects near the horizon to be nearer than those high in the sky; and, hence, we expect them to appear larger. Another theory holds that we must consider the sky to be like a flattened vault and that this accounts for the apparent size of the moon at the horizon. Still another theory holds that the illusion is produced by atmospheric conditions. At the moment, no one view seems wholly adequate in its explanation of this natural visual illusion.

See also AMBIGUOUS FIGURES, IMPOSSIBLE FIGURES, and PERSPECTIVE PARADOXES.

THE PARADOX OF VOTING

It has often been suggested that to avoid the problem of having the candidate with a minority of the popular vote win the United States presidential election by winning a majority of the electoral vote, the voting procedure for electing the President of the United States should be changed to a direct popular vote. By this method, the candidate who receives the most number of popular votes would always win the election. Obviously, however, this procedure does not necessarily mean that a candidate with a minority of the vote cannot win. For example, it is quite possible that in a four-way race the percentage of votes for each candidate could be such that a minority candidate, one who receives much less than a majority of the vote, actually wins the election. Consider, for instance, a hypothetical four-way race in which each of two liberal candidates gets 29 percent of the vote, the moderate candidate gets 12 percent, and the conservative gets 30 percent. It would be difficult to show that the majority of voters got its way in such a situation, for fully 70 percent of the population voted for someone other than the winner.

Numerous methods for overcoming this problem have been suggested. A favorite among these suggestions is the idea of requiring a runoff election between the top two vote getters when no one wins a clear majority, that is, more than 50 percent. Yet, this suggestion has its problems, as we can see in the example of a three-way race between a liberal, a moderate, and a conservative. Let us suppose that in the election, the liberal candidate takes 45 percent of the vote, the moderate takes 13 percent, and the conservative 42 percent. We know the preference scale of each type of voter: liberal voters prefer the liberal candidate to the moderate candidate and the moderate candidate to the conservative candidate. The conservative voters prefer the conservative candidate to the moderate candidate and the moderate to the liberal. The moderates are split in their preferences. Of the 13 percent, 11 percent prefer the moderate over the liberal candidate and the liberal candidate over the conservative one. The other 2 percent of the moderate voters prefer the moderate to the conservative candidate and the conservative to the liberal candidate. In a two-way election between the top two vote getters, it is the liberal candidate who would win, with a total of 56 percent of the vote (Figure 110). Does this outcome represent the will of the majority of those who cast their votes?

Three-Way Race	Liberal 45%		Moderate 13%		Conservative 42%	
Two-Way Races						
Liberal versus Conservative	45% 11% 56%	(Liberal) (Moderate) (Total)			42% 2% 44%	(Conservative) (Moderate) (Total)
Moderate versus Liberal	45%	(Liberal)	13% 42% 55%	(Moderate) (Conservative) (Total)		
Moderate versus Conservative			13% 45% 58%	(Moderate) (Liberal) (Total)	42%	(Conservative)

110. The paradox of voting. Notice that the moderate candidate in pairwise races against either the liberal candidate or the conservative candidate wins the election. Yet, in the three-way race it is the moderate candidate who is excluded from the runoff race.

Most people's immediate reaction to the above question is that, of course, the vote represents the will of the majority. After all, 56 percent of the people voted for the liberal candidate, whereas only 44 percent voted for the conservative. But consider what would happen if the moderate candidate ran against the liberal in the runoff election. In this case, the moderate would get 55 percent of the vote (assuming he gets all the conservative votes based on their preference scale), and the liberal candidate would get only 45 percent of the vote. Likewise, in a pairwise contest against the conservative candidate, the moderate will win again (in this case he gets all the liberal votes) with 58 percent of the total vote. How then can we say that the will of the majority has truly been served by the runoff between the liberal and the conservative candidates?

The paradox of voting was first discovered by the Marquis de Condorcet, an eighteenth-century French political philosopher and mathematician. It was a popular subject of discussion among nineteenth-century mathematicians and logicians, including Lewis Carroll. The paradox was rediscovered in the late 1940s by the Canadian economist Duncan Black and became an integral part of the work of the American Nobel Prize-winning (1972) economist Kenneth Arrow.

Arrow formulated five basic conditions that he believed are essential to any democracy. These conditions were succinctly presented for the general reader by Morton Davis, a professor of mathematics at the City College of New York in his 1980 book *Mathematically Speaking:*

1. *The decision-making procedure must yield a unique preference order.*

Whatever the preferences of society's members, the procedure should come up with one and only one preference order for society.

2. *Society should be responsive to its members.*

The more the individuals in a society like an alternative, the more the society should like it too. Suppose a decision-making procedure yields a preference order for society on the basis of its members' preferences in which alternative X is preferred to Y. If the individual preference orders were changed so that some liked X even better but Y just the same, then in the new preference order society should still prefer X to Y.

3. *Society's choice between two alternatives is based on its members' choices between those two alternatives (and not any others).*

Suppose society prefers X to Y and people change their minds about other alternatives but not about X and Y. Then X should still be preferred to Y. Society's decision about whether X is better than Y shouldn't depend on its decision about whether U is better than V.

4. The decision-making procedure should not prejudge.

For any two alternatives X and Y, there must be some possible individual preferences that would allow society to prefer X to Y. Otherwise, Y is automatically preferred to X and the group preferences are unresponsive to those of its members.

5. There is no prejudgment by an individual.

Arrow assumes there is no dictator, that is, society's choices are not identical to the choices of any single individual. If this condition didn't have to be satisfied, it would be easy enough to find a voting mechanism, but Arrow wouldn't consider it representative of the individuals in the whole group.

These conditions are considered by almost all commentators to be perfectly reasonable requirements for any democratic method of decision making based on expressing individual preference by means of voting. What Arrow demonstrated was that a perfect democratic voting system—that is, one in which the majority's choice always wins—is impossible without violating one of the five basic conditions. As noted by another American Nobel Prize-winning economist (1970), Paul Samuelson, and other commentators on the problem, Arrow's proof has had as significant an impact on political science and economics as have the German Kurt Gödel's incompleteness theorems on mathematical thought.

The cause of the paradox of voting is rooted in the nature of transitive and non-transitive relations. A transitive relation is defined as follows: if the relation holds between the first element and the second element and between the second element and the third element, then the relation also holds between the first and third elements. For example, if X is older than Y and Y is older than Z, then it is safe to assume that X is older than Z.

However, not all relations are transitive. For instance, if X hates Y and Y hates Z, we cannot conclude that X hates Z, because hate is not a transitive relation. In the case of the paradox of voting, individual preferences are transitive, but this transitivity cannot be transferred from the individuals to the group of voters in a society by means of any system that involves majority-rule voting on pairs of candidates.

It is this fact which makes it possible in the three-way election shown in Figure 110 and discussed above to eliminate the moderate candidate, even though he would defeat either of the two other candidates in a two-way election. In other words, although the ranking of the candidates is transitive for an individual, the society's ranking is non-transitive: a majority prefers X to Y, and a majority prefers Y to Z, but a majority prefers Z to X and not, as we would expect, X to Z.

Arrow actually showed that the paradox of voting is not dependent on any one voting system. Any system that involves adding transitive individual preferences and that satisfies the five basic conditions is subject to the paradox. Only by rejecting one or several of Arrow's principles of democracy (which social scientists are hesitant to do) can the paradox be avoided. Most often, the suggestion has been made that a dictator—that is, a judge or arbitrator—be chosen by lot to make a decision when the voting system is unable to produce a clear-cut majority winner.

Numerous empirical examples of the paradox of voting have been discussed by social scientists, and the paradox has been shown to have strategic political implications. Consider, for example, a bill for federal aid for school construction which was introduced in the United States House of Representatives in 1956. According to William H. Riker, an American political scientist, the House in this case was faced with three alternatives: the original bill which called for aid for school construction, an amended bill which prohibited federal aid to states that had segregated schools, and no bill at all.

According to Riker, there were three groups of voters in the House in this situation. The first group, which consisted mostly of southern Democrats, wanted the original bill passed. Their preference scale was the original bill, no bill, and the amended bill. The second group, consisting mostly of northern Democrats, had a preference scale of the amended bill (they were for school integration), the original bill, and no bill. The third group, which consisted mostly of Republicans, had a preference scale of no bill, the amended bill, and the original bill.

The House of Representatives uses a voting system that is called the "amendment," or "tournament," procedure. In this procedure, if the amendment is passed, then the second vote is between the amended bill and no bill. If on the first vote the amendment is defeated, then the second vote is between the original bill and no bill. In the case of the federal-aid-for-school-construction bill, the amended bill passed on the first vote because, according to Riker, the Republicans (who preferred no school-aid bill) voted with the northern Democrats for the amended bill. They did this so that the second vote would be between the amended bill and no bill. In the second vote, the Republicans switched their votes, and no bill was passed!

In Riker's example, the Republicans engaged in what is called "sophisticated voting"—voting which prevents a voter's worst possible outcome from occurring. In the case of the Republican representatives, the worst possible outcome was the original bill. By voting for the amended bill, the Republicans made certain that their worst possible choice could not occur; the second vote was between the amended bill and no bill. If the Republicans had voted their true preference, that is, had they voted sincerely, they would have had to deal with the original bill on the second vote and it probably would have passed. Instead, by engaging in sophisticated voting, they achieved their goal.

Since the work done by Duncan Black and Kenneth Arrow, the paradox of voting has become the most famous and widely discussed paradox of the social sciences. Some commentators have been very distressed by the idea that an undesirable candidate may be forced upon the citizens of a democracy because of the paradox of voting. Critics of this view have argued that the paradox of voting, despite the abstruse mathematical analyses it has generated, is of little consequence in the real world. Nevertheless, some research shows that the greater the number of voters or the greater the number of candidates, the more likely it is that the paradox will occur.

The essence of the paradox of voting is that there is no ironclad transformation of individual preferences into society's preferences. We see this type of inconsistency between the individual's choices and the society's choices in many everyday situations. Society spends much more money on weapons than on the education of its youth; yet, if we polled the individuals in the society, the vast majority would certainly have a reversed preference. As the American political scientist Steven Brams notes in his book *Paradoxes in Politics*, "Probably the most important lesson of the paradox of voting is that not only is there a qualitative difference between individual and social choice, but—on reflection—one should not expect otherwise."

See also STATISTICAL REVERSAL PARADOXES.

ZENO'S PARADOXES

Imagine a racecourse that stretches 1 kilometer from point A to point B. Then imagine a runner—call him Achilles—who starts at point A and runs at a uniform rate of 1 meter per second toward his goal, point B. Now, consider these facts: Achilles must first traverse half the distance between points A and B, arriving midway between the two points, at what has been labeled point C. Then Achilles must travel half the remaining distance between point C and his goal, B, arriving at point D. This halving process continues ad infinitum, because regardless of how little distance remains to be crossed, it can still be halved (Figure 111).

Furthermore, each finite segment of the racecourse requires a finite length of time to be traversed; and, since we are dealing with an infinite number of finite intervals, we must conclude that Achilles will never reach his goal. What is wrong with the reasoning in this argument?

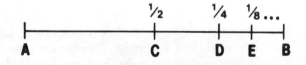

111. Zeno's paradox of the racecourse, I.

This argument is the first of four paradoxes of motion attributed to the Greek philosopher Zeno of Elea, who lived in the fifth century B.C. Very little is known about Zeno. He was probably born about 490 B.C., and he is thought to have written his paradoxes—

approximately forty in all—about 465 B.C. Fewer than two hundred of Zeno's actual words have survived, and of these, there are a few references to only two paradoxes. All our information about Zeno's paradoxes of motion is from Aristotle, who wrote about them the following century in his *Physics,* and from other early commentators such as Simplicius, who lived in the sixth century A.D. and who may have had a summary of Zeno's original work.

Aristotle acknowledges Zeno as the father of the dialectic, a method of argumentation in which one debater sets forth a proposition while another disproves it by showing that it leads to a contradiction. Zeno's dialectic method, which was used by Socrates and other philosophers and which had great influence on the nature of philosophical debate in ancient Greece, provides an essential part of the context for understanding his paradoxes of motion.

Zeno was a student of the Greek philosopher Parmenides, who believed that the universe was a solid, uniform, motionless, and unchanging sphere. Parmenides' views were really attacks on the beliefs held by the Ionian philosophers, most notably Heraclitus of Ephesus, who argued that the world is in a state of constant change or flux—that the river we step in today is not the river we step in tomorrow—and the views of Pythagoras, who claimed that the basic irreducible material of which the universe is composed is numbers.

According to Parmenides, it is possible to make three different statements about the "basic stuff" of which the universe is made: (1) *It* is, (2) *It* is not, (3) *It* both is and is not. The last statement can be dismissed as a contradiction. The second statement runs into problems because, according to the Parmenidean view, one cannot really talk about the absence of *It* while also using terms to describe *It.* Thus, we are left with "*It* is." Zeno's paradoxes of motion can be seen as attempts to defend Parmenides' views by showing that the views of his opponents—such as the Pythagoreans—led to absurdities.

To return to the paradox of the racecourse—or, the paradox of the dichotomy, as it is also called—we can see that its intent was to demonstrate that the idea of motion along a continuum leads to logically contradictory results. For although we know that the runner can reach the end of the racecourse, in fact, we cannot prove this logically. Where, then, is the fallacy in Zeno's argument? Or is there one?

It took mathematicians and philosophers almost two thousand years to find a generally—though not completely—acceptable solution to Zeno's paradox of the racecourse. The solution, if accepted, seems to indicate that Zeno was mistaken in his notions about the sums of infinite series. As we noted earlier in our discussion of the Infinite Hotel paradox, some infinite series, such as the set of all even integers, have no sum; that is, one can always add another term so that the sum grows larger and larger, ad infinitum. Thus, if we take the infinite series of all even integers ($0 + 2 + 4 + 6 + 8 + 10 + 12 \ldots$), we can always increase the final sum by adding another integer. An infinite series is said to be divergent if the sequence of its partial sums diverges, as does this one. An infinite series that diverges has no sum.

However, this is not the case with all infinite series. Consider the infinite series involved in Zeno's paradox of the racecourse. This series can be represented as

$$\tfrac{1}{2} + \tfrac{1}{4} + \tfrac{1}{8} + \tfrac{1}{16} + \tfrac{1}{32} \ldots$$

It is self-evident that this series is also infinite, for we can always add a smaller fraction by halving the preceding one. An infinite series is said to be convergent if and only if the sequence of its partial sums converges, as it does in this series. The limit S of the sequence of partial sums is called the sum of the series. In this case the limit is 1, for the more terms you add to the series the closer the sum approaches the limit 1. (The Dutch artist M. C. Escher's woodcut *Square Limit*, shown in Figure 112, presents a visual analogy to the concept of an infinite series that converges to a limit.)

Thus, assuming a uniform rate of motion of 1 meter per second, we can conclude that Achilles will traverse the 1-kilometer racecourse in 1,000 seconds. The fallacy in Zeno's paradox of the racecourse is the idea that the sum of an infinite number of finite intervals of space or time must be infinite. Once again, our intuitive notions about infinity have led us astray.

Zeno's paradox of the racecourse was presented in another version—if not by Zeno, then by some other ancient Greek. This second version was intended to show that it was impossible for Achilles ever to begin his race. Consider, for example, the fact that Achilles must first reach the midway point (C) between the starting point (A) and his goal (B). But, before he can do this, he must reach the midway point between A and C, and so on, ad infinitum

112. Square Limit, *by M. C. Escher. The largest fishlike creatures in the center go through a radial reduction process as they move outward toward infinity—all within the context of the boundaries of a square.*

(Figure 113). There is always an infinity of points between any two points on a continuum. Thus, Achilles can never leave his starting point, because there is no next point. We are dealing with the same infinite series, and it still has a limit of 1.

Zeno's second paradox of motion, of Achilles and the tortoise, is probably the best known of his four paradoxes of motion. In this problem, the fleet Greek warrior runs a race against a slow-moving tortoise. Assume Achilles runs at ten times the speed of the tortoise (1 meter per second to 0.1 meter per second). The tortoise is given

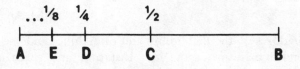

113. Zeno's paradox of the racecourse, II.

a 100-meter handicap in a race that is 1,000 meters. By the time Achilles reaches the tortoise's starting point T_0, the tortoise will have moved on to point T_1. Soon, Achilles will reach point T_1, but by then the tortoise would have moved on to T_2, and so on, ad infinitum (Figure 114). Every time Achilles reaches a point where the tortoise has just been, the tortoise has moved on a bit. Although the distances between the two runners will diminish rapidly, Achilles can never catch up with the tortoise, or so it would seem.

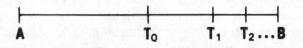

114. Zeno's paradox of Achilles and the tortoise.

It is not uncommon at this point to protest Zeno's logic and to counterattack, using one's real experiences with races. However, this is not the problem that Zeno's paradox poses. Zeno requires that we find the logical flaw in his argument. As in the case of the two versions of the dichotomy paradox, we are dealing here with an infinite series that has a limit. Based on the ten-to-one speed ratio in this version of the paradox, the series involved is $100 + 10 + 1 + \frac{1}{10} + \ldots$, and it approaches the limit 111.1. Thus, at exactly $111\frac{1}{9}$ meters Achilles will be in a dead heat with the tortoise, and from this moment on he will always be ahead of the creature.

As the British philosopher Bertrand Russell notes in his essay "The Problem of Infinity Considered Historically":

> This argument is essentially the same as the previous one [for the dichotomy]. It shows that, if Achilles ever overtakes the tortoise, it must be after an infinite number of instants have elapsed since he started. This is in fact true; but the view that an infinite number of instants makes up an infinitely long time is not true, and therefore the conclusion that Achilles will never overtake the tortoise does not follow.

The paradoxes of the dichotomy and of Achilles and the tortoise seem intended to disprove the idea that time and space are continuous. Zeno's other two paradoxes of motion—the paradoxes of the arrow and of the stadium—seem intended to disprove the opposite idea; that is, that time and space are composed of discrete "atoms," each of which is irreducible. The paradoxes of the arrow and the stadium can be construed as attempts to refute the notion that time is composed of "atoms" of no duration and that space is composed of "atoms" of no size. If we substitute "instants" for "atoms" of time and "points" for "atoms" of space, we have a fairly modern mathematical description of time and space.

In the paradox of the arrow, Zeno asks us to consider an arrow in flight and argues that, in fact, the arrow must always be at rest. At each instant the arrow occupies a space equal to itself. Movement is impossible, because an instant by definition has no parts. If the arrow were capable of moving during an instant, we would contradict the definition of an instant, for the arrow would be in one position during the first part of the instant and in another position in the other part of the instant. Thus, the arrow never seems to be moving but rather, as Russell notes in his essay on infinity, "in some miraculous way the change of position has to occur *between* the instants, that is to say, not at any time whatever." If the arrow does not move at any given instant, how then does it make its flight?

The solution to the paradox of the arrow is a bit more complex than those to the dichotomy and of Achilles and the tortoise. In the paradox of the arrow, the argument assumes that there is a time continuum and that it is like the space continuum. Both are assumed to be discrete and atomistic in nature; for every point along the arrow's path, there is a corresponding instant. Aristotle dismissed Zeno's argument by denying that time is a continuum consisting of indivisible instants. However, today it is Aristotle's analysis that is rejected by almost all contemporary mathematicians and philosophers. As we noted earlier, the modern view is that space and time are both continua of the same type.

We know that the points along the continuum of a line are densely ordered; that is, between any two points there is always another point and, thus, an infinity of other points. The same is true of instants along the time continuum: between any two instants there is an infinity of other instants. It is true that one can traverse an infinite set of points in a finite time, and one can even know that an infinity of instants has passed in a finite interval of time. The German mathematician Georg Cantor's theory of transfinite numbers provides insight into the nature of the problem posed in Zeno's paradox of the arrow, but it does not resolve the paradox on a practical level. The fundamental paradox seems to remain: *how* does the arrow get from one end of its course to the other, if at every instant it is stationary?

To fully resolve the paradox it is necessary to examine carefully our notions about the nature of motion. Most people believe they have a firm grasp on what motion is, based on their real-world experience and their intuition. An object is in motion if at one instant it is in one position and in the next instant it is in another position. An object at rest, in comparison, is in one position one instant and in the same position in the next instant. Our experience and intuition lead us to believe that motion is some force or power that the object possesses as it moves along its path.

The modern mathematical view of the motion does not support what our experience and intuition tell us. According to modern mathematics, motion *is* considered simply as a series of stops. As Bertrand Russell notes in his book *The Principles of Mathematics*,

> . . . we must entirely reject the notion of a *state* of motion. Motion consists merely in the occupation of different places at different times. . . . There is no transition from place to place, no consecutive moment, no such thing as velocity except in the sense of a real number which is the limit of a certain set of quotients.

The following example may help to dispel the sense of unreality that the mathematical view of motion might first appear to create. Imagine that you are on a blanket on a beach and that a beach ball rolls by you. You happen to have a camera, and you take a picture of the ball as it passes. Later, you find the beach ball and you bring it back to the exact spot that it occupied when you took the first picture of it rolling by you. Then, you take a second photograph of the stationary beach ball. When the pictures are developed, they are identical; there are no telltale clues in the background to indicate which photograph shows the beach ball in motion and which shows the beach ball at rest. How can the two photographs be distinguished from each other? In fact, they can't be distinguished from each other.

In other words, Zeno's argument in the paradox of the arrow is correct in a sense. There is no such thing as a *state* of motion; at every instant the moving arrow or the moving beach ball is where it is, in a position equal to itself. This position is mathematically no different than if the arrow or the beach ball were at rest in the same position. But motion requires a *duration* of time and an instant by definition has no duration. It is here that the paradox turns to fallacy: although there is no such thing as a state of motion, one cannot conclude from this that there is no such thing as motion. Motion requires a series of positions and instants, not just one of each. Using the methods of calculus, modern mathematics has developed a static theory of motion able to describe movement such as that exhibited by the arrow or the beach ball without the need for a state of motion or for fixed infinitesimals.

It is not uncommon to hear practical objections to the argument in the paradox of the arrow. For example, when we drive a car and look at the speedometer, don't we have an indication of how fast the car is traveling at that instant? Why, then, is there no such thing as a state of motion? While it is true that a speedometer provides a measure of the instantaneous velocity of the car, it is not true that the instantaneous velocity of the car is a measure of how fast the car is traveling at that instant. Instantaneous velocity is really a measure of the limit of average velocities during intervals converging to zero and always containing the given instant. The important thing to remember about instantaneous velocity is that it is a purely static, geometrical measurement.*

---

* The calculus allows us to give two different histories of the motion of the arrow or the beach ball. (This assumes we put aside all practical questions concerning gravity, air currents, and the like. Mathematics does have answers for these questions, too, but the methods involved are beyond the scope of this book.) One history is the object's distance history and the other is its velocity history. The distance history tells us where on its path the arrow or the beach ball is at every moment. The velocity history tells us how fast the arrow or the beach ball is moving at each instant. Either history taken alone provides a complete description of the object's motion. The problem of translating one type of graph history into the other is a basic problem of the calculus. The graph showing the velocity history of the object is called the derivative of the graph showing the object's distance history, and the graph

An analogy can be made between the modern mathematical view of motion and the frames of a piece of film showing the motion of an object. The real film represents the motion of an object in a finite number of frames, but according to the modern mathematical view, there is an infinite number of such "frames" possible between any two instants of the arrow's flight. In practice, a mathematician also uses only a finite number of intervals in his calculations of an object's motion. The methods of the modern mathematical view of motion do provide practical, accurate answers, not only to Zeno's paradoxes of motion but also to real-world problems that involve motion, but they do not provide a real definition of motion itself.

Of Zeno's four paradoxes of motion, the paradox of the stadium is probably the least discussed. Many commentators dismiss the problem as trivial, for it is based on an obvious mathematical fallacy. Imagine that it is half time at a collegiate football game and that the fans are being entertained by the home team's cheering committee, which consists of three trumpet players, three baton-twirling cheerleaders, and three drummers. They are arranged in three rows as shown in Figure 115.

At the sound of the trumpets' first middle C, two of the rows move. The trumpet players stand still, while the cheerleaders and the drummers move toward each other at the same speed until they

---

showing the distance history of the object is called integral of the graph showing the object's velocity history.

It is easy to imagine how we could gather information for the distance history of a moving object, but how would we go about obtaining information for its velocity history? That depends on which type of velocity we are dealing with. If the object travels at a constant velocity, then all we need to do is calculate the average velocity by taking the distance the object traveled and dividing by the time it took to travel that distance. Thus, if the object traveled a straight line path of 100 yards in 10 seconds, then its average velocity would be 10 yards per second. However, in the real world few objects move at a constant velocity; certainly, neither Zeno's arrow nor our beach ball would qualify as an object moving at a constant velocity.

If we assume that the object's velocity will change during different intervals of time, then the job of calculating its velocity at each instant becomes more complex. As we noted above, to do this we must calculate the instantaneous velocity of the object. The instantaneous velocity of an object is defined as the slope of the tangent line at the corresponding point on the graph showing the distance history of the object, if such a tangent line can be constructed.

Trumpet Players	T_1	T_2	T_3
Cheerleaders	C_1	C_2	C_3
Drummers	D_1	D_2	D_3

115. First position in Zeno's stadium paradox.

$$T_1 \quad T_2 \quad T_3$$

$$C_1 \quad C_2 \quad C_3$$

$$D_1 \quad D_2 \quad D_3$$

116. Second position in Zeno's stadium paradox.

achieve the position shown in Figure 116, wherein all the members of each row align.

Consider what has happened in this situation. By the time the members of each row are aligned, the first drummer, D_1, would have passed twice as many cheerleaders as he did trumpet players. After all, D_1 aligns with T_1 by moving one unit to the left. For D_1 to align with C_1, he must pass by two cheerleaders. Zeno concluded that since it took the same amount of time for C_1 and D_1 to align with T_1 and since D_1 passes twice as many cheerleaders as trumpet players, then half the time must be equal to double the time. The conclusion is somewhat vague, but this is how Zeno stated it.

Assuming an ordinary analysis of the physics of the situation, Zeno's problem does appear to be based on a simpleminded fallacy, for it does not account for differences in the relative speeds of the people involved. As noted in the discussion of time paradoxes, the speed—or, more strictly speaking, the velocity—of A relative to B is calculated by adding their velocities. Thus, in the stadium paradox C_1's velocity relative to D_1 is twice as great as C_1's velocity relative to T_1.

While the matter seems simple to resolve once we have defined the concept of relative velocity, the paradox is subject to other interpretations. Several philosophers, including Russell and the British philosopher G. E. Owen, maintain that there is a way to view the stadium paradox that will generate further unexpected and troublesome problems in logic. Consider, for example, the following explication of this Russell-Owen interpretation made by the American logician Wesley Salmon in his introduction to *Zeno's Paradoxes*, a collection of essays he edited:

> Suppose, as people occasionally do, that space and time are atomistic in character, being composed of space-atoms and time-atoms of nonzero size, rather than being composed of points and instants whose size is zero. Under these circumstances, motion would consist in taking up different discrete locations at different discrete instants. Now, if we suppose that the [trumpet players] are not moving, but the [cheerleaders] move to the [right] at the rate of one place per instant while the [drummers] move to the left at the same speed, some of the [drummers] get past some of the [cheerleaders] without ever passing them. $[D_1]$ begins at the right of $[C_2]$ and $[D_1]$ ends up at the left of $[C_2]$, but there is no instant at which $[D_1]$ lines up with $[C_2]$; consequently, there is no time at which they pass each other—it never happens.

The solutions to Zeno's paradoxes that have been presented so far are the "accepted" solutions, meaning that they are accepted by most mathematicians and a good number of philosophers. However, there are many notable thinkers—the Englishman Alfred North Whitehead, the Frenchman Henri Bergson, and the American Max Black, to name a few—who, while agreeing with the mathematics to some extent, nevertheless find unresolved difficulties lurking in Zeno's paradoxes of motion.

For example, according to Black, the real problem does not consist in finding the sum of an infinite series but in determining if either Achilles or the tortoise really can be said to have completed an infinite series of tasks in a finite time, as implied in the mathematical solution to the problem. Black and other commentators have created infinity machines to explain their views. Among the most famous of these strange creations is an infinity lamp postulated by the British philosopher James Thomson.

The Thomson lamp is not a real object; it is a thought experiment. Like most study lamps, it has a single on-off button somewhere on its base. You turn the lamp on by pushing the button;

and, if it is on, you turn it off by pushing the same button. Now, imagine that a person begins by turning the lamp on, taking exactly one minute to make his finger push the button and to light the bulb. The person then switches off the lamp in a half of a minute, and then turns it on again in a quarter of a minute, and so on ad infinitum, each new push taking half the time as the preceding one. Thomson calls the completion of an infinite series of such tasks a "supertask."

Putting aside all objections to physical impossibilities—that is, assuming such a lamp (and such a bulb) can be built and assuming that it is physically possible for someone to complete the infinite series of switching operations—would the lamp be on or off at the end of a two-minute period? (Remember, a series can contain an infinite number of terms—or, in this case, operations—even though it has a two-minute limit.) In fact, the lamp cannot be on, because after an infinite series of switches, every time it was on it was immediately shut off. The opposite is also true, for in an infinite series of switches, each time the lamp is off, it subsequently is turned on. Thus, the lamp is either on and off, or it is neither on nor off!

This result becomes apparent if we give values to the various lamp positions, reserving 0 for off and 1 for on. Thus, every time the lamp is turned on, we add one ($+ 1$), and every time it is turned off, we subtract one ($- 1$). The question then becomes what is the value of the sum of the infinite series $+ 1 - 1 + 1 - 1 + 1 \ldots$ at the end of two minutes? Such a series has no fixed sum; instead, mathematicians describe it as oscillating between two values. If this is so, we might suspect that the inventors of infinity machines are correct and that it is logically impossible to complete such a supertask and, by analogy, logically impossible for Achilles to complete the tasks set before him in Zeno's paradoxes.

Fortunately, such dire consequences do not necessarily result from the Thomson lamp and other infinity machines. As the American mathematician Paul Benacerraf has noted, all the mathematics is saying is that for any time prior to $t = 2$ minutes, we can determine if the lamp is on or off, but for t itself no value can be fixed. This should not surprise us because an infinite series has no last term. Nor does it imply the contradictions described earlier; it merely indicates that we may logically conclude nothing or anything about the state of the lamp two minutes after the experiment or at any time thereafter.

There appears to be a significant difference between the supertasks described in the Thomson lamp thought experiment and Achilles' movement in the paradox of the racecourse. Achilles' run is assumed to be continuous, whereas the Thomson lamp experiment involves discontinuous actions that form an aleph-null set, to use Cantor's term.

As Cantor showed, any line segment, regardless of its size, has more than an aleph-null infinity of points. But these points are unextended; that is, they have no dimension—their magnitude equals zero. How then can we say a line segment is an *extended* continuum if it consists only of unextended points—even if it consists of an infinity of them? Nothing added to nothing is still nothing. The problem just raised is really a contemporary view of Zeno's paradox of plurality, which many commentators consider to be his most significant problem.

In the paradox of plurality, Zeno argued that if any extended thing exists, it must consist of parts. Since parts can be subdivided indefinitely, each extended thing must contain an infinity of parts. Furthermore, these ultimate parts must be unextended, for if they were extended they would be subject to further subdivision. But, concludes Zeno, if this is so, then how can any extended thing exist? After all, if we add parts of no magnitude, we are back to adding nothings.

In a very real sense, Zeno's paradox of plurality underlies all his paradoxes of motion. If it cannot be resolved satisfactorily, then the logical and mathematical—if not the physical—problems of the paradoxes of motion remain. The significance of the paradoxes of plurality for Achilles and the racecourse and for Achilles and the tortoise is self-evident: in these paradoxes we are dealing with a physical continuum. But, the paradox of plurality also applies to the arrow and the stadium, for mathematicians view the temporal continuum as an infinite series of unextended instants; that is, instants without duration.

Is it then just a simple case of mathematical theory being unable to represent accurately continuous motion such as that exhibited by Achilles and the arrow? Yes and no. Yes, because it is true that the mathematical concept of the continuum, though consistent within formal systems of mathematics, fails to provide a totally adequate description of motion as we experience it in the real world. No, because, as the American mathematician Adolf Grünbaum has shown in his mathematical and scientific analyses of Zeno's paradoxes, it is possible to construct a discontinuous analogue to the continuous motions of Achilles or the arrow.

Grünbaum asks us to imagine a second Achilles, who runs parallel to the first in the initial version of the paradox of the racecourse. The original Achilles Grünbaum calls the "legato" Achilles, and the second he calls the "staccato" Achilles. The descriptive labels refer to the type of motion each performs. The legato Achilles motion is, as in the original paradox, continuous. The staccato Achilles runs twice as fast as his legato counterpart, thereby covering the first half of the racecourse in half the time it takes the legato Achilles. But upon reaching the midpoint, the staccato Achilles then rests for a period of time equal to the one he just ran. At the moment the legato Achilles catches up, the staccato Achilles instantaneously takes off again at twice the velocity of the legato Achilles, and reaches the next midpoint in half the time. The staccato Achilles pauses for the appropriate time until the legato Achilles reaches him, and so on, ad infinitum.

Now, we already know that the legato Achilles completes the course when the infinite series described in the paradox converges to its limit of 1. But what about the staccato Achilles? By the terms of the problem he will arrive at the finish line at the same time as the legato Achilles. Yet, if this is so, then the staccato Achilles has actually performed an infinite series of discrete tasks in a finite period of time! With this outcome in mind can we really say that the Thomson lamp and other infinity machines are logically impossible or that the method for finding the limit of an infinite series that converges really resolves Zeno's paradoxes of motion? These are questions that are still being pondered.

Zeno's paradoxes of plurality and motion also raise metaphysical problems. As Wesley Salmon notes, William James, the American philosopher, and Whitehead both argued that Zeno's paradoxes provided the ultimate proof that all temporal processes are by nature discontinuous. Whitehead viewed the physical universe as an extended space-time continuum, pieces of which come into existence as a whole entity or not at all. (This has obvious parallels with the

French physicist Louis de Broglie's comments about the nature of four-dimensional space-time, discussed above in the chapter on time paradoxes.) According to Whitehead, it is only after becoming that we can view the piece or entity as infinitely divisible; the act of becoming is itself indivisible.

This brings us back to the paradox of Amphibius, which we now can see is really Zeno's paradox of plurality disguised as a metaphysical paradox of becoming. In theory, an infinite number of frames could be photographed between any two instants of Amphibius' development from tadpole to frog (using an infinity camera, of course), and we would still never find the frame in which it is a frog and which is preceded by a frame in which it is a tadpole. The American philosopher James Cargile's view of Amphibius' development has its parallels to Whitehead's atomistic view of becoming and to Bergson's cinematographic view of becoming. Bergson believed in a real continuity of becoming (unlike Whitehead), but he claimed that we are intellectually incapable of understanding it. According to Bergson, we must enter the process of change if we are to gain some insight into its real nature. Bergson believed that the direct perception of becoming was beyond mathematical or logical analysis and that we could experience it directly only by metaphysical intuition.

As might be expected, the views of Whitehead and Bergson are not without their critics. Grünbaum for one has provided mathematical and logical analyses of Zeno's paradoxes which not only argue that the mathematics of the continuum is accurate, but also show that the mathematics of the continuum is consistent with reality. Grünbaum's solution to the problem involves mathematical and scientific concepts well beyond the scope of this book, and it has proven to be highly controversial, departing radically as it does from "standard" solutions.

Based on our discussion, it would seem that every time a "solution" is found to Zeno's paradoxes of motion, other problems arise. Salmon makes precisely this point in the following wise and homely analogy from the conclusion of the introduction to *Zeno's Paradoxes:*

> Zeno's paradoxes have an onion-like quality; as one peels away outer layers by disposing of the more superficial difficulties, new

and more profound problems are revealed. For instance, as we show that it is mathematically consistent to suppose that an infinite series of positive terms has a finite sum, the problem of the infinity machines arises. When we show how the infinity machines can be handled, the problem of composing the continuum out of unextended elements appears. When charges concerning the consistency of the continuum are met, the problem of identity of structure between the mathematical continuum and the continuum of physical times confronts us. And so on. Will we ever succeed in stripping away all of the layers and providing a complete resolution of all the difficulties that arise out of Zeno's paradoxes? And if we should succeed, what would be left in the center? In a certain sense, nothing, it would seem. We will not find a metaphysical nutmeat such as Whitehead's atomism, or any other fundamental truth about the nature of reality. However, we should not conclude that nothing of value remains. The layers we have peeled away have in them the elements of a nourishing philosophical broth. The analysis itself, dealing in detail with a host of fundamental problems, is richly rewarding in terms of our understanding of space, time, motion, continuity, and infinity. We would be foolish indeed to conclude that the onion was nothing but skin, and to discard the whole thing as worthless.

It would, of course, be rash to conclude that we had actually arrived at a complete resolution of all problems that come out of Zeno's paradoxes. Each age, from Aristotle on down, seems to find in the paradoxes difficulties that are roughly commensurate with the mathematical, logical, and philosophical resources then available. When more powerful tools emerge, philosophers seem willing to acknowledge deeper difficulties that would have proved insurmountable for more primitive methods. We may have resolutions which are appropriate to our present level of understanding, but they may appear quite inadequate when we have advanced further. The paradoxes do, after all, go to the very heart of space, time, and motion, and these are profoundly difficult concepts.

Or, has the onion infinitely many layers? If so, we may be faced with an infinite sequence of tasks that does defy completion in a finite time, for the steps become longer, not shorter, as the difficulties become deeper.

See also THE PARADOX OF AMPHIBIUS and THE INFINITE HOTEL PARADOX.

BIBLIOGRAPHY

AMBIGUOUS FIGURES

Bloomer, Carolyn M. *Principles of Visual Perception.* New York: Van Nostrand Reinhold, 1976.

Gardner, Martin. "Optical Illusions." In *Mathematical Circus.* New York: Random House, Vintage Books, 1981. Pp. 3–15.

Gregory, Richard L. *The Intelligent Eye.* New York: McGraw-Hill, 1970.

———. "Human Perception" and "The Effect of Touch on a Visually Ambiguous Three-Dimensional Figure." In *Concepts and Mechanisms of Perception.* New York: Scribner, 1974. Pp. 50–64, 282–89.

Kim, Scott. *Inversions.* Peterborough, N.H.: Byte Books, 1981.

Lewitt, Sol. *Incomplete Open Cubes.* New York: John Weber Gallery, 1974.

Luckiesh, M. *Visual Illusions: Their Causes, Characteristics, and Applications.* 1922. Reprint. New York: Dover, 1965.

Newell, Peter. *Topsys & Turvys.* 1902. Reprint. New York: Dover, 1964.

Whistler, Rex, and Laurence Whistler. *Aha!* 1946. Reprint. Boston: Houghton Mifflin, 1979.

THE PARADOX OF AMPHIBIUS

Baum, Robert. *Logic.* New York: Holt, Rinehart and Winston, 1975. Pp. 443–47, 477–79.

Campbell, Richmond. "The Sorites Paradox." *Philosophical Studies* 26 (1975): 175–91.

Cargile, James. "The Sorites Paradox." *British Journal for the Philosophy of Science* 20 (1969): 193–202.

Edlow, R. Blair. "The Stoics on Ambiguity." *Journal of the History of Philosophy*, October 1975: 423–35.

Ehlers, Henry J. *Logic: Modern and Traditional*. Columbus, O.: Merrill, 1976. Pp. 82–91, 190–201.

Fogelin, Robert J. *Understanding Arguments*. New York: Harcourt Brace Jovanovich, 1978. Pp. 73–94.

THE BARBER PARADOX

Gardner, Martin. "Logical Paradoxes." *Antioch Review*, Summer 1963: 481–86.

Intisar, Ul-Haque. "Russell on Paradoxes." In *A Critical Study of Logical Paradoxes*. Peshawar, Pakistan: Peshawar University Press, n.d. Pp. 1–35, 52–63.

Quine, Willard V. "New Foundations." In *From a Logical Point of View*. 2d ed. New York: Harper & Row, 1961. Pp. 80–101.

———. "The Ways of Paradox." In *The Ways of Paradox and Other Essays*. New York: Random House, 1966. Pp. 1–18.

Russell, Bertrand. *The Principles of Mathematics*. 2d ed. New York: Norton, 1943.

Van Heijenoort, John. "Logical Paradoxes." In *The Encyclopaedia of Philosophy*, Vol. 5. New York: Macmillan/Free Press, 1967. Pp. 45–51.

THE CROCODILE'S DILEMMA

Bartley, William Warren III, ed. *Lewis Carroll's Symbolic Logic*. New York: Clarkson N. Potter, 1977. Pp. 425, 436–38.

Burnyeat, M. F. "Protagoras and Self-refutation in Later Greek Philosophy." *The Philosophical Review*, January 1976: 49–69.

Goossens, W. K. "Euathlus and Protagoras." *Logique et Analyse*, March–June 1977: 67–75.

Lenzen, Wolfgang. "Protagoras versus Euathlus: Reflections on a So-called Paradox." *Ratio*, December 1977: 176–80.

Smullyan, Raymond. "From Paradox to Truth." In *What Is the Name of This Book?* Englewood Cliffs, N.J.: Prentice-Hall, 1978. Pp. 213–24.

M. C. ESCHER'S PARADOXES

Coxeter, H. S. M. "Two-dimensional Crystallography." In *Introduction to Geometry*. New York: Wiley, 1961. Pp. 50–66.

Ernst, Bruno. *The Magic Mirror of M. C. Escher*. New York: Random House, 1976.

Gardner, Martin. "The Art of M. C. Escher." In *Mathematical Carnival*. New York: Random House, Vintage Books, 1977. Pp. 89–102.

Locher, J., ed. *The World of M. C. Escher*. New York: Abrams, 1971.

Ranucci, Ernest R. "Master of Tessellation: M. C. Escher, 1898–1972." *Mathematics Teacher*, April 1974: 299–306.

Teuber, Marianne L. "Sources of Ambiguity in the Prints of M. C. Escher." *Scientific American*, July 1974: 90–104.

GEOMETRIC VANISHES

Fisher, John, ed. *The Magic of Lewis Carroll*. New York: Simon and Schuster, 1973. Pp. 92–97.

Gardner, Martin. "Geometric Vanishes." In *Mathematics, Magic, and Mystery*. New York: Dover, 1956. Pp. 114–55.

Stover, Mel. "The Disappearing Man and Other Vanishing Paradoxes." *Games*, November–December 1980: 14–18.

Weaver, Warren. "Lewis Carroll and a Geometrical Paradox." *American Mathematical Monthly* 45 (1938): 234–36.

THE GRUE-BLEEN PARADOX

Cohen, Yael. "A New View of Grue." *Zeitschrift für Allgemeine Wissenschaftstheorie* 10 (1979): 244–52.

Feyerabend, Paul K. "A Note on Two 'Problems' of Induction." *British Journal for the Philosophy of Science* 19 (1968): 251–53.

Foster, Laurence. "Feyerabend's Solution to the Goodman Paradox." *British Journal for the Philosophy of Science* 20 (1969): 259–60.

Gardner, Martin. "On the Fabric of Inductive Logic and Some Probability Paradoxes." *Scientific American*, March 1976: 119–22.

Goodman, Nelson. *Fact, Fiction, and Forecast*. 2d ed. Indianapolis: Bobbs-Merrill, 1965. Pp. 63–126.

Hesse, Mary. "Ramifications of 'Grue.'" *British Journal for the Philosophy of Science* 20 (1969): 13–25.

Hunt, G. M. K. "Further Ramifications of 'Grue.'" *British Journal for the Philosophy of Science* 20 (1969): 257–58.

Kahane, Howard. "Eliminative Confirmation and Paradoxes." *British Journal for the Philosophy of Science* 20 (1969): 160–62.

Konyndyk, Kenneth, Jr. "Solving Goodman's Paradox: A Reply to Stemmer." *Philosophical Studies*, April 1980: 297–305.

Lin, Chao-tien. "Solutions to the Paradoxes of Confirmation, Goodman's Paradox, and Two New Theories of Confirmation." *Philosophy of Science* 45 (1968): 415–19.

Priest, Graham. "Gruesome Simplicity." *Philosophy of Science* 43 (1976): 432–37.

Salmon, Wesley C. "Confirmation." *Scientific American*, May 1973: 75–83.

Stemmer, Nathan. "A Partial Solution to the Goodman Paradox." *Philosophical Studies* 34 (1978): 177–85.

THE HETEROLOGICAL PARADOX

Cargile, James. "Semantic Paradoxes." In *Paradoxes: A Study of Form and Predication*. London: Cambridge University Press, 1979. Pp. 226–302.

Dumitriu, Anton. "The Logico-mathematical Antinomies: Contemporary and Scholastic Solutions." *International Philosophical Quarterly*, September 1974: 309–28.

———. "The Solution of Logico-mathematical Paradoxes." *International Philosophical Quarterly*, March 1969: 63–100.

Gardner, Martin. "Logical Paradoxes." *Antioch Review*, Summer 1963: 172–77.

Gregory, Joshua C. "Heterological and Homological." *Mind* 61 (1952): 85–88.

Grelling, Kurt. "The Logical Paradoxes." *Mind* 45 (1936): 481–86.

Intisar, Ul-Haque. *A Critical Study of Logical Paradoxes*. Peshawar, Pakistan: Peshawar University Press, n.d. Pp. 16–20, 47–56.

Northrop, Eugene P. "Vicious Circles: Paradoxes in Logic." In *Riddles in Mathematics*. London: English Universities Press, 1946. Pp. 199–201.

Quine, Willard V. "The Ways of Paradox." In *The Ways of Paradox and Other Essays*. New York: Random House, 1966. Pp. 1–18.

Teensma, E. *The Paradoxes*. Assen, Netherlands: Van Gorcum, 1969. Pp. 25–26, 34–35.

Van Heijenoort, John. "Logical Paradoxes." In *The Encyclopaedia of Philosophy*, Vol. 5. New York: Macmillan/Free Press, 1967. P. 47.

Whitehead, Alfred N., and Bertrand Russell. *Principia Mathematica*. 2d ed. London: Cambridge University Press, 1962. Pp. 60–64.

IMPOSSIBLE FIGURES

Coxeter, H. S. M. "Four-dimensional Geometry." In *Introduction to Geometry*. New York: Wiley, 1961. Pp. 396–412.

Ernst, Bruno. *The Magic Mirror of M. C. Escher*. New York: Random House, 1976.

Gardner, Martin. "Optical Illusions." In *Mathematical Circus*. New York: Random House, Vintage Books, 1981. Pp. 3–15.

Gregory, Richard L. "The Confounded Eye." In Richard L. Gregory and E. H. Gombrich, eds. *Illusion in Nature and Art*. New York: Scribner, 1973. Pp. 49–95.

———. *The Intelligent Eye.* New York: McGraw-Hill, 1970.

———. "Perceptual Illusions and Brain Models." In *Concepts and Mechanisms of Perception.* New York: Scribner, 1974. Pp. 357–79.

Kim, Scott E. "An Impossible Four-dimensional Illusion." In David W. Brisson, ed. *Hypergraphics: Visualizing Complex Relationships in Art, Science and Technology.* Boulder, Col.: Westview Press, 1978. Pp. 186–239.

Penrose, L. S., and R. Penrose. "Impossible Objects: A Special Type of Illusion." *British Journal of Psychology* 49 (1958): 31–33.

THE INFINITE HOTEL PARADOX

Benardete, J. A. *Infinity: An Essay in Metaphysics.* London: Oxford University Press, 1964.

Bunch, Bryan H. "Paradoxes that Count." In *Mathematical Fallacies and Paradoxes.* New York: Van Nostrand Reinhold, 1982. Pp. 110–39.

Dretske, Fred I. "Counting to Infinity." *Analysis* 25 (1964–65): 99–101.

Gamow, George. *One, Two, Three . . . Infinity.* 1947. Reprint. New York: Bantam Books, 1961. Pp. 14–24.

Gardner, Martin. "The Hierarchy of Infinities and the Problems It Spawns." *Scientific American,* March 1966: 112–16.

———. "The Infinite Regress in Philosophy, Literature, and Mathematical Proof." *Scientific American,* April 1965: 128–32.

———. "Some Paradoxes and Puzzles Involving Infinite Series and the Concept of Limit." *Scientific American,* November 1964: 126–28.

Kasner, Edward, and James R. Newman. "Beyond the Googol." In *Mathematics and the Imagination.* New York: Simon and Schuster, 1967. Pp. 27–64.

Kline, Morris. "The Paradoxes of the Infinite." In *Mathematics in Western Culture.* London: Oxford University Press, 1953. Pp. 395–409.

Northrop, Eugene P. "Outward Bound: Paradoxes of the Infinite." In *Riddles in Mathematics.* London: English Universities Press, 1946. Pp. 117–65.

Péter, Rózsa. *Playing with Infinity*. 1957. Reprint. New York: Dover, 1976. Pp. 137–53.

Reid, Constance. *From Zero to Infinity*. 3d ed. New York: Crowell, 1964.

Rucker, Rudy. *Infinity and the Mind*. Boston: Birkhäuser, 1982.

Sondheimer, Ernst, and Alan Rogerson. *Numbers and Infinity*. London: Cambridge University Press, 1981.

Thomson, James. "Infinity in Mathematics and Logic." In *The Encyclopaedia of Philosophy*, Vol. 3. New York: Macmillan/Free Press, 1967. Pp. 183–90.

THE LAWYERS' PARADOX

Burnyeat, M. F. "Protagoras and Self-refutation in Later Greek Philosophy." *The Philosophical Review*, January 1976: 49–69.

Goossens, W. K. "Euathlus and Protagoras." *Logique et Analyse*, March–June 1977: 67–75.

Lenzen, Wolfgang. "Protagoras versus Euathlus: Reflections on a So-called Paradox." *Ratio*, December 1977: 176–80.

Smullyan, Raymond. "From Paradox to Truth." In *What Is the Name of This Book?* Englewood Cliffs, N.J.: Prentice-Hall, 1978. Pp. 213–24.

THE LIAR PARADOX

Ashworth, E. J. "The Treatment of the Semantic Paradoxes from 1400 to 1700." *Notre Dame Journal of Formal Logic*, January 1972: 34–51.

———. "Will Socrates Cross the Bridge? A Problem in Medieval Logic." *Franciscan Studies* 14 (1976): 75–83.

Brennan, Joseph G. "The Nature of Logical Truth." In *A Handbook of Logic*. 2d ed. New York: Harper & Row, 1961. Pp. 155–65.

Cervantes Saavedra, Miguel de. *The Adventures of Don Quixote*. Trans. J. M. Cohen. Harmondsworth, England: Penguin Books, 1951. Pp. 797–99.

Dumitriu, Anton. "The Logico-mathematical Antinomies: Contemporary and Scholastic Solutions." *International Philosophical Quarterly*, September 1974: 309–28.

Ezorsky, Gertrude. "Performative Theory of Truth." In *The Encyclopaedia of Philosophy*, Vol. 6. New York: Macmillan/Free Press, 1967. Pp. 172–78.

Gardner, Martin. "Logical Paradoxes." *Antioch Review*, Summer 1963: 172–77.

Grelling, Kurt. "The Logical Paradoxes." *Mind* 45 (1936): 481–86.

Haack, Susan. "Paradoxes." In *Philosophy of Logics*. London: Cambridge University Press, 1978. Pp. 135–51.

Hofstadter, Douglas R. *Gödel, Escher, Bach: An Eternal Golden Braid.* New York: Basic Books, 1979.

Intisar, Ul-Haque. "The Liar Paradox." In *A Critical Study of Logical Paradoxes*. Peshawar, Pakistan: Peshawar University Press, n.d. Pp. 64–93.

Kahane, Howard. "Logical Paradoxes." In *Logic and Philosophy*. Belmont, Cal.: Wadsworth, 1973. Pp. 310–15.

Kripke, Saul. "Outline of a Theory of Truth." *Journal of Philosophy*, November 6, 1975: 690–716.

Lewis, C. I., and C. H. Langford. "The Logical Paradoxes." In *Symbolic Logic*. 2d ed. New York: Dover, 1959. Pp. 438–85.

Michael, Emily. "Pierce's Paradoxical Solution to the Liar's Paradox." *Notre Dame Journal of Formal Logic*, July 1975: 369–74.

Mostowski, Andrzej. "Alfred Tarski." In *The Encyclopaedia of Philosophy*, Vol. 8. New York: Macmillan/Free Press, 1967. Pp. 77–81.

Nagel, Ernest, and James R. Newman. *Gödel's Proof.* New York: New York University Press, 1958.

Parsons, Charles. "The Liar Paradox." *Journal of Philosophical Logic*, October 1974: 381–412.

Prior, A. N. "Correspondence Theory of Truth." In *The Encyclopaedia of Philosophy*, Vol. 2. New York: Macmillan/Free Press, 1967. Pp. 223–32.

Quine, Willard V. "The Ways of Paradox." In *The Ways of Paradox and Other Essays*. New York: Random House, 1966. Pp. 1–18.

Rucker, Rudy. "Gödel's Incompleteness Theorems." In *Infinity and the Mind*. Boston: Birkhäuser, 1982. Pp. 272–94.

Smullyan, Raymond. "Gödel's Discovery." In *What Is the Name of This Book?* Englewood Cliffs, N.J.: Prentice-Hall, 1978. Pp. 225–41.

Spade, Paul V., ed. *Peter of Ailly: Concepts and Insolubles*. Dordrecht, Netherlands: D. Reidel, 1980.

———. *William Heytesbury's "On Insoluble Sentences."* Toronto: Pontifical Institute of Mediaeval Studies, 1979.

———. *The Mediaeval Liar: A Catalog of the Insolubilia Literature*, Toronto: Pontifical Institute of Mediaeval Studies, 1975.

Tarski, Alfred. "On Undecidable Statements in Enlarged Systems of Logic and the Concept of Truth." *Journal of Symbolic Logic* 4 (1939): 105–12.

———. "Truth and Proof." *Scientific American*, June 1969. 63–77.

———. "The Semantic Conception of Truth and the Foundations of Semantics." *Journal of Philosophy and Phenomenological Research* 4 (1939): 341–75.

Teensma, E. *The Paradoxes*. Assen, Netherlands: Van Gorcum, 1969. Pp. 18–25.

Ushenko, A. P. "A Note on the Liar Paradox." *Mind* 64 (1955): 543.

Van Heijenoort, John. "Logical Paradoxes." In *The Encyclopaedia of Philosophy*, Vol. 5. New York: Macmillan/Free Press, 1967. Pp. 45–51.

———. "Gödel's Theorem." In *The Encyclopaedia of Philosophy*, Vol. 3. New York: Macmillan/Free Press, 1967. Pp. 348–57.

PERSPECTIVE PARADOXES

Bloomer, Carolyn B. *Principles of Visual Perception*. New York: Van Nostrand Reinhold, 1976.

Descargues, Pierre. *Perspective*. New York: Abrams, 1977.

Ernst, Bruno. "Explorations into Perspective." In *The Magic Mirror of M. C. Escher*. New York: Random House, 1976. Pp. 42–57.

Gombrich, E. H. "Ambiguities of the Third Dimension." In *Art and Illusion: A Study in the Psychology of Pictorial Representation*. 2d ed. Princeton: Princeton University Press. Bollingen Paperback, 1972. Pp. 242–87.

Gregory, Richard L. *The Intelligent Eye*. New York: McGraw-Hill, 1970.

———. "Seeing in Depth." In *Concepts and Mechanisms of Perception*. New York: Scribner, 1974. Pp. 333–41.

Leeman, Fred, Joost Elffers, and Mike Schuyt. *Hidden Images: Games of Perception, Anamorphic Art, and Illusion from the Renaissance to the Present*. Trans. Ellyn Childs Allison and Margaret L. Kaplan. New York: Abrams, 1976.

Luckiesh, M. *Visual Illusions: Their Causes, Characteristics, and Applications*. 1922. Reprint. New York: Dover, 1965.

THE PREDICTION PARADOX

Brams, Steven J. "A Paradox of Prediction." In *Paradoxes in Politics: An Introduction to the Nonobvious in Political Science*. New York: Free Press, 1976. Pp. 193–213.

Gardner, Martin. "Free-will Revisited, with a Mind-bending Prediction Paradox by William Newcomb." *Scientific American*, July 1973: 104–8.

Howard, Nigel. *Paradoxes of Rationality: The Theory of Metagames and Political Behavior*. Cambridge, Mass.: MIT Press, 1971.

Kaplan, David, and Richard Montague. "A Paradox Regained." *Notre Dame Journal of Formal Logic*, July 1960: 79–90.

Meltzer, B., and I. J. Good. "Two Forms of the Prediction Paradox." *British Journal for the Philosophy of Science* 16 (1965): 50–51.

Nozick, Robert. "Newcomb's Problem and Two Principles of Choice." In Nicholas Rescher, ed. *Essays in Honor of Carl G. Hempel*. Dordrecht, Netherlands: D. Reidel, 1970. Pp. 114–46.

Watzlawick, Paul. "Imaginary Communication." In *How Real Is Real? Confusion, Disinformation, Communication.* New York: Random House, Vintage Books, 1977. Pp. 207–16.

Windt, Peter Y. "The Liar in the Prediction Paradox." *American Philosophical Quarterly,* January 1973: 65–68.

THE PRISONER'S DILEMMA

Brams, Steven J. "The Paradox of Cooperation." In *Paradoxes in Politics: An Introduction to the Nonobvious in Political Science.* New York: Free Press, 1976. Pp. 79–111.

Davis, Morton. "Games Adults Play: Game Theory." In *Mathematically Speaking.* New York: Harcourt Brace Jovanovich, 1980. Pp. 154–99.

Howard, Nigel. *Paradoxes of Rationality: The Theory of Metagames and Political Behavior.* Cambridge, Mass.: MIT Press, 1971.

Rapoport, Anatol. "Escape from Paradox." *Scientific American,* July 1967: 50–56.

———. and Albert M. Chammah. *The Prisoner's Dilemma: A Critical Study in Conflict and Cooperation.* Ann Arbor: University of Michigan Press, 1965.

Watzlawick, Paul. "Interdependence." In *How Real Is Real? Confusion, Disinformation, Communication.* New York: Random House, Vintage Books, 1977. Pp. 97–105.

PROBABILITY PARADOXES

Baum, Robert. "Probability." In *Logic.* New York: Holt, Rinehart and Winston, 1975. Pp. 385–405.

Davis, Morton. "Method in Our Madness: Probability." In *Mathematically Speaking.* New York: Harcourt Brace Jovanovich, 1980. Pp. 48–105.

Gamow, George. *One, Two, Three . . . Infinity.* 1947. Reprint. New York: Bantam Books, 1961. Pp. 207–23.

Gardner, Martin. "On the Fabric of Inductive Logic, and Some Probability Paradoxes." *Scientific American,* March 1976: 119–22.

———. "Probability Paradoxes." In *Mathematical Puzzles and Diversions*. New York: Simon and Schuster/Fireside, 1959.

———. "Why the Long Arm of Coincidence Is Usually Not as Long as It Seems." *Scientific American*, October 1972: 110–12.

Kahane, Howard. "Probability." In *Logic and Philosophy*. Belmont, Cal.: Wadsworth, 1973. Pp. 266–81.

Kasner, Edward, and James R. Newman. "Chance and Chanceability." In *Mathematics and the Imagination*. New York: Simon and Schuster, 1967. Pp. 223–64.

Northrop, Eugene P. "What Are the Chances?: Paradoxes in Probability." In *Riddles in Mathematics*. London: English Universities Press, 1946. Pp. 166–95.

Stoppard, Tom. *Rosencrantz and Guildenstern Are Dead*. New York: Grove Press, 1967.

THE RAVEN PARADOX

Carnap, Rudolf. *Logical Foundations of Probability*. Chicago: University of Chicago Press, 1962.

———. "Truth and Confirmation." In Marguerite H. Foster and Michael L. Martin, eds. *Probability, Confirmation, and Simplicity*. New York: Odyssey Press, 1966. Pp. 137–44.

Gardner, Martin. "On the Fabric of Inductive Logic and Some Probability Paradoxes." *Scientific American*, March 1976: 119–22.

Hempel, Carl G. "Studies in the Logic of Confirmation." In Marguerite H. Foster and Michael L. Martin, eds. *Probability, Confirmation, and Simplicity*. New York: Odyssey Press, 1966. Pp. 145–83.

Kahane, Howard. "Eliminative Confirmation and Paradoxes." *British Journal for the Philosophy of Science* 20 (1969): 160–62.

———. *Logic and Philosophy*. Belmont, Cal.: Wadsworth, 1973. Pp. 306–9.

Luckenbach, Sidney A., ed. *Probabilities, Problems, and Paradoxes: Readings in Inductive Logic*. Encino, Cal.: Dickenson, 1972.

Salmon, Wesley C. "Confirmation." *Scientific American*, May 1973: 75–83.

Srzednicki, Jan. "The Two Paradoxes of Induction." *Dialectics and Humanism*, Spring 1976: 150–64.

THE SHOPKEEPER'S PARADOX

Bartley, William Warren III, ed. *Lewis Carroll's Symbolic Logic*. New York: Clarkson N. Potter, 1977. Pp. 442–65.

Baum, Robert. *Logic*. New York: Holt, Rinehart and Winston, 1975. Pp. 162–67.

Burks, Arthur W., and Irving M. Copi. "Lewis Carroll's Barber Shop Paradox." *Mind* 59 (1950): 219–22.

Haack, Susan. *Philosophy of Logics*. London: Cambridge University Press, 1978. Pp. 35–38, 170–203.

Johnson, W. E. "Hypotheticals in a Context." *Mind* 4 (1895): 143–44.

———. "A Logical Paradox." *Mind* 3 (1894): 583.

Kahane, Howard. *Logic and Philosophy*. Belmont, Cal.: Wadsworth, 1973. Pp. 21–24, 82–85.

Russell, Bertrand. *The Principles of Mathematics*. London: Allen & Unwin, 1903.

Sidgwick, Alfred. "Hypotheticals in a Context." *Mind* 4 (1895): 543.

———. "A Logical Paradox." *Mind* 3 (1894): 580.

Wilson, John Cook. "Lewis Carroll's Logical Paradox." *Mind* 190 (1905): 292–93.

STATISTICAL REVERSAL PARADOXES

Bickel, P. J., E. A. Hamel, and J. W. O'Connell. "Sex Bias in Graduate Admissions: Data from Berkeley." *Science*, February 7, 1975: 398–403.

Blyth, Colin R. "On Simpson's Paradox and the Sure-things Principle" and "Some Probability Paradoxes in Choice from Among Random Alternatives." *Journal of the American Statistical Association*, June 1972: 364–73.

Gardner, Martin. "On the Fabric of Inductive Logic and Some Probability Paradoxes." *Scientific American*, March 1976: 119–22.

Salmon, Wesley C. "Confirmation." *Scientific American*, May 1973: 75–83.

TIME PARADOXES

Benford, G. A., D. L. Book, and W. A. Newcomb. "The Tachyonic Antitelephone." *Physical Review D.: Particles and Fields*, July 15, 1970: 263–65.

Capra, Fritjof. *The Tao of Physics*. New York: Bantam Books, 1977. Pp. 147–73.

Einstein, Albert. *Relativity: The Special and General Theory*. 1916. Reprint. New York: Crown, 1961.

Gardner, Martin. *The Ambidextrous Universe: Mirror Asymmetry and Time-reversed Worlds*. 2d ed. New York: Scribner, 1979.

———. "Can Time Go Backward?" *Scientific American*, January 1967: 98–108.

———. "On Altering the Past, Delaying the Future, and Other Ways of Tampering with Time." *Scientific American*, March 1979: 21–27.

———. "On the Contradictions of Time Travel . . ." *Scientific American*, May 1974: 120–23.

———. *The Relativity Explosion*. New York: Random House, Vintage Books, 1976. Pp. 35–72, 127–40.

Lewis, David. "The Paradoxes of Time Travel." *American Philosophical Quarterly*, April 1976: 145–52.

Park, David. *The Image of Eternity*. New York: New American Library, 1980.

Russell, Bertrand. *The ABC of Relativity*. London: Allen & Unwin, 1958.

Zukav, Gary. *The Dancing Wu Li Masters*. New York: Morrow, 1979. Pp. 156–207, 230–57.

TOPOLOGICAL PARADOXES

Barr, Stephen. *Experiments in Topology.* New York: Crowell, 1964.

Coxeter, H. S. M. "Topology of Surfaces." In *Introduction to Geometry.* New York: Wiley, 1961. Pp. 379–95.

Gardner, Martin. "Klein Bottles and Other Surfaces." In *The Sixth Book of Mathematical Games from Scientific American.* San Francisco: Freeman, 1971. Pp. 9–18.

———. "Möbius Bands." In *Mathematical Magic Show.* New York: Knopf, 1977. Pp. 123–35.

Kasner, Edward, and James R. Newman. "Rubber Sheet Geometry." In *Mathematics and the Imagination.* New York: Simon and Schuster, 1967. Pp. 265–98.

Khurgin, Ya. "Rubber-sheet Mathematics." In *Did You Say Mathematics?* Trans. George Yankowsky. Moscow: Mir Publishers, 1974. Pp. 41–70.

Northrop, Eugene P. "Now You See It—Now You Don't: Paradoxes in Geometry." In *Riddles in Mathematics.* London: English Universities Press, 1946. Pp. 47–76.

Tymoczko, Thomas. "The Four-Color Problem and Its Philosophical Significance." *Journal of Philosophy,* February 1979: 57–83.

THE UNEXPECTED EXAMINATION PARADOX

Bosch, Jorge. "The Examination Paradox and Formal Prediction." *Logique et Analyse,* September–December 1972: 505–25.

Gardner, Martin. "The Unexpected Hanging." In *The Unexpected Hanging and Other Mathematical Diversions.* New York: Simon and Schuster, Fireside Book, 1969. Pp. 11–23.

Medlin, Brian. "The Unexpected Examination." *American Philosophical Quarterly,* January 1964: 66–72.

Meltzer, B. "The Third Possibility." *Mind* 73 (1964): 430–33.

O'Beirne, T. H. "Can the Unexpected Never Happen?" *The New Scientist,* May 25, 1965: 464–65.

O'Connor, D. J. "Pragmatic Paradoxes." *Mind* 57 (1948): 358–59.

———. "Pragmatic Paradoxes and Fugitive Propositions." *Mind* 60 (1951): 536–38.

Quine, Willard V. "On a So-called Paradox." *Mind* 62 (1953): 65–67.

Scriven, Michael. "Paradoxical Announcements." *Mind* 60 (1951): 403–7.

Wright, Crispin, and Aidan Sudbury. "The Paradox of the Unexpected Examination." *Australasian Journal of Philosophy*, May 1977: 41–58.

VISUAL ILLUSIONS

Bloomer, Carolyn M. *Principles of Visual Perception*. New York: Van Nostrand Reinhold, 1976.

Gardner, Martin. "Optical Illusions." In *Mathematical Circus*. New York: Random House, Vintage Books, 1981. Pp. 3–15.

Gregory, Richard L. *The Intelligent Eye*. New York: McGraw-Hill, 1970.

———. "Human Perception." In *Concepts and Mechanisms of Perception*. New York: Scribner, 1974. Pp. 50–64.

Lanners, Edi, ed. *Illusions*. Trans. Heinz Norden. New York: Holt, Rinehart and Winston, 1977.

Luckiesh, M. *Visual Illusions: Their Causes, Characteristics, and Applications*. 1922. Reprint. New York: Dover, 1965.

Paraquin, Charles H. *Eye Teasers: Optical Illusion Puzzles*. New York: Sterling, 1977.

THE PARADOX OF VOTING

Brams, Steven J. "The Paradox of Voting." In *Paradoxes in Politics: An Introduction to the Nonobvious in Political Science*. New York: Free Press, 1976. Pp. 29–51.

Davis, Morton. "To Pick and Choose: An Application to Voting." In *Mathematically Speaking*. New York: Harcourt Brace Jovanovich, 1980. Pp. 202–32.

Fishburn, Peter C. "Paradoxes of Voting." *American Political Science Review*, June 1974: 537–46.

Gardner, Martin. "On the Paradoxical Situations That Arise from Nontransitive Relations." *Scientific American*, October 1974: 120–25.

Niemi, Richard G., and William H. Riker. "The Choice of Voting Systems." *Scientific American*, June 1976: 21–27.

Riker, William H. "Arrow's Theorem and Some Examples of the Paradox of Voting." In John M. Claunch, ed. *Mathematical Applications of Political Science*. Dallas: Arnold Foundation of Southern Methodist University, 1969. Pp. 41–60.

ZENO'S PARADOXES

Bergson, Henri. "The Cinematographic View of Becoming." In Wesley C. Salmon, ed. *Zeno's Paradoxes*. Indianapolis: Bobbs-Merrill, 1970. Pp. 59–66.

Black, Max. "Zeno's Paradoxes." In *Problems of Analysis*. 1954. Reprint. Westport, Conn.: Greenwood Press, 1971. Pp. 93–154.

Booth, N. "Zeno's Paradoxes." *Journal of Hellenic Studies* 77, 2 (1957): 187–201.

Gardner, Martin. "Further Encounters with Touching Cubes and the Paradoxes of Zeno as 'Supertasks.'" *Scientific American*, December 1971: 96–99.

———. "Some Paradoxes and Puzzles Involving Infinite Series and the Concept of Limit." *Scientific American*, November 1964: 126–28, 133.

Grünbaum, Adolf. *Modern Science and Zeno's Paradoxes*. Middletown, Conn.: Wesleyan University Press, 1967.

Kline, Morris. "The Paradoxes of the Infinite." In *Mathematics in Western Culture*. 1953. Reprint. London: Oxford University Press, 1976. Pp. 395–409.

Northrop, Eugene P. "Outward Bound: Paradoxes of the Infinite." In *Riddles in Mathematics*. London: English Universities Press, 1946. Pp. 117–23.

Russell, Bertrand. "The Problem of Infinity Considered Historically." In Wesley C. Salmon, ed. *Zeno's Paradoxes*. Indianapolis: Bobbs-Merrill, 1970. Pp. 45–58.

Salmon, Wesley C., ed. *Zeno's Paradoxes*. Indianapolis: Bobbs-Merrill, 1970.

Schlegel, Richard. "Quantum Mechanics and the Paradoxes of Zeno." *American Scientist* 36 (1948): 396–402, 414.

Siegel, Rudolph. "The Paradoxes of Zeno and Some Similarities Between Ancient Greek and Modern Thought." *Janus* 48 (1959): 24–47.

Thomson, James. "Tasks and Super-Tasks." In Wesley C. Salmon, ed. *Zeno's Paradoxes*. Indianapolis: Bobbs-Merrill, 1970. Pp. 89–102.

Ushenko, Andrew. "Zeno's Paradoxes." *Mind* 55 (1946): 151–65.

Vlastos, Gregory. "Zeno of Elea." In *The Encyclopaedia of Philosophy*, Vol. 8. New York: Macmillan/Free Press, 1967. Pp. 369–79.

Whitehead, Alfred N. *Process and Reality*. New York: Macmillan, 1929.

INDEX